Altair SLC

The SAS Language Compiler

Philip R Holland

Altair SLC: The SAS Language Compiler

Copyright © 2025, Philip R Holland, Royston, Herts, UK

ISBN: 978-1-326-75547-8

All rights reserved.

First edition, June 2024.
Second edition, May 2025.
Reprinted, June 2025.

SAS® and all other SAS Institute Inc. product or service names are registered trademarks or trademarks of SAS Institute Inc. in the USA and other countries. ® indicates USA registration.

SAS is also used to refer to the SAS language, a public domain programming language that requires no licence and is free for anyone to use.

Other brand and product names are registered trademarks or trademarks of their respective companies.

Table of Contents

Preface..6
    About the Author...7
    Acknowledgements..8
    Reviews..9

SAS Programming Alternatives...10

What is Altair SLC?...11
    Introduction..11
    How can Altair SLC be accessed?..11
    Supported platforms in 2024..12
    Supported platforms in 2025..13
    Altair SLC and the Output Delivery System (ODS)..............14
        ODS DOCUMENT and PROC DOCUMENT example.....15
    Visual Studio Code Editor (VS Code): Altair SLC extension 20
    Conclusions...21

Introduction to Altair Analytics Workbench...........................22
    Introduction..22
    Analytics Workbench 2024...22
        Supported platforms in 2024..22
        Initial View..23
    Analytics Workbench 2025...30
        Supported platforms in 2025..30
        Initial View..30
    Differences from Interactive SAS, Enterprise Guide and SAS Studio..37
        What is a Workspace?...37
        Setting the Current Working Folder.................................39
        Associating File Types...40
        Assigning an Altair SLC Server..42
        Running SAS Programs...42
        Customising Workbench..44
    Conclusions...46

Altair SLC for Clinical Trials...47
   Introduction...47
   Chapter Glossary..47
   The Rules of Clinical Trlals Programming.........................48
   Configuring Altair SLC..48
   Useful Input Data Sets..49
   Macro to Standardise and Compare ADaM Data Sets........50
   Over to You!...52
   How Did You Get On?...53
   Conclusions..53

Generating Graphics with Altair SLC.....................................54
   Introduction...54
   How Many Ways to Create Graphs?...............................54
      SAS/GRAPH..54
      ODS Graphics 'SG' Procedures...................................55
      ODS Graphics with Graph Templates..........................55
   Scatter Plots..56
   Line Plots...57
   Regression Plots..59
   Error Bar Plots...61
   Box Plots..64
   Vertical Bar Charts...66
      Simple Vertical Bar Charts..67
      Stacked Vertical Bar Charts..68
      Clustered Vertical Bar Charts......................................70
   Horizontal Bar Charts...72
      Simple Horizontal Bar Charts......................................72
      Stacked Horizontal Bar Charts....................................74
      Clustered Horizontal Bar Charts..................................76
   2D Pie Charts..78
   Conclusions...82

Using Altair SLC with R and Python.......................................83
   Introduction...83
   SAS Software and R...83

    Program Flow...84
    Coding Issues..89
    Altair SLC and R Software Environment.............................90
        Differences between SAS Software and Altair SLC.........90
        Program Flow...90
    Altair SLC and Python Software Environment....................93
        Program Flow...94
    Conclusions..100

Recommended Reading..102

    Web Links...102

Alphabetical Index...103

Preface

When selecting a technical book for myself I tend to choose one where there are lots of examples and sample code snippets that I can use and adapt for my own development projects. I wanted to write a book that I could use for reference myself, so I have tried to make sure there are code snippets wherever possible.

The book is devoted to Altair SLC, and where it is similar to and different from SAS software.

Code samples are provided throughout this book, so you can learn more about Altair SLC and SAS programming by following these examples.

About the Author

For 43 years Philip R Holland has been working with SAS software. In that time he has witnessed the evolution of the software from a mainframe-only system to an analytics platform used in all of the major business sectors on all the major platforms.

Philip R Holland has advised a broad range of clients in the UK, throughout Europe and the United States as an independent consultant and founder of Holland Numerics Limited, a SAS technical consultancy. A SAS user since 1981, he has worked on all the major computing platforms that support SAS software, and he frequently speaks on a wide range of topics related to SAS at conferences around the globe.

He is the editor of VIEWS News, the quarterly journal of the VIEWS International SAS Programming Community, and has been a VIEWS committee member since 2002. He is a SAS Certified Advanced Programmer, a member of the British Computer Society, and a Chartered Information Technology Practitioner.

Acknowledgements

My wife, Angela, for her tolerance and encouragement.

LeRoy Bessler, for his absolutely thorough proof-reading, even though his English is American, and mine is native British!

Don Henderson, who suggested new content to support what I had already written.

Pablo Orosco Joerger for his assistance with the Altair SLC chapters and programs.

Bartosz Jabłoński for his insights into the more obscure features of SAS software.

Nico Chart and Oliver Robinson (Altair) for their comments and observations about Altair SLC.

Reviews

Phil has used SAS on all of the platforms, mainframe, UNIX, and Windows. If Mac was a platform, Phil would take you as reader there, too. He takes you to Altair SLC, R, and Python, where you can be a user of the SAS language, and those two ever more popular adjuncts to SAS, without the expense of a SAS licence, and clarifies the differences between SAS Software and Altair SLC. The book includes a graphics capabilities tour with the various tools in its scope. Nowhere else available is the chapter devoted to Altair SLC for Clinical Trials, which is like a book-guided Hands-On Workshop self-help get-acquainted tutorial. The book will take you to places that nobody else would take you. Explore it and explore SAS.

LeRoy Bessler, Bessler Consulting and Research

SAS Programming Alternatives

This section includes chapters about alternatives to programming using the SAS System:

- Altair SLC, formerly known as WPS from World Programming, can interpret and run the majority of SAS programs, as well as run Python and R code. Altair has developed the application separately from SAS, so it will never be 100% compatible, as updates have to be written and tested after SAS software changes are published.

- In order to demonstrate the compatibility of Altair SLC and SAS software, I have collected some of the programming examples I have published in this and previous books, and the results when run in Altair SLC will be discussed.

- Microsoft's Visual Studio Code Editor (VSCode) now has an Altair SLC extension that can edit SAS programs, and then submit them to a local or remote Altair SLC server.

What is Altair SLC?

Introduction

In the past, WPS from World Programming has provided an alternative to the SAS System by offering a competing compiler that can successfully run SAS language code. However, until quite recently that proportion has not included ODS Graphics, where my recent programming interests have been focused. After Altair bought World Programming and settled the long-running dispute with the SAS Institute, progress in supporting SAS language syntax for ODS Graphics has accelerated.

Altair SLC, the new name of WPS, is run in an Eclipse IDE (Interactive Development Environment), which supports multiple platforms including Windows, Mac and Linux. The single product licence includes many of the components for which SAS Institute requires separate licences, like graphics, database integration, statistics, time series and operations research. The licence subscription also costs less than that for SAS Institute software, but, of course, you are getting less functionality, albeit most of the needed features are present, because Altair SLC is constantly improving. However, Altair SLC product licence also includes access to Python and R programming modules, which can be used in any program. This means any missing SAS Institute language support could be replaced by code using another programming language.

While SAS-compatibility is probably around 90%, database access is extensive.

How can Altair SLC be accessed?

There are several licensing models used by Altair:

- Community or Personal Licence:

    - This is a free licence including Altair Analytics Workbench, which uses the Eclipse IDE.

- Academic and Student Licence:

    - Details can be found at **https://altair.com/academic-program**.

- Other licences are paid-for:

  ○ Any paid-for licence includes Altair Analytics Workbench, which uses the Eclipse IDE.

- Command line access to Altair SLC is also available, but not using the Community Licence, using the following syntax, analogous to the SAS command line syntax:

wps [<program-file-name>] <options> where:

<options> can be a list of either:

-<optionname> [<optionvalue>]

-config <config-file-name>

-set <env-var-name> <env-var-value>

Supported platforms in 2024

Altair SLC is supported on the following platforms*:

- **Taken from https://help.altair.com/2024/SLC/Altair-SLC-New-in-Release-en.pdf

  - AIX version 7.2 or later running on PowerPC (ppc)/POWER/System p hardware.

  - Microsoft Windows version 10 or later running on x86_64 hardware.

  - Microsoft Windows Server 2016 or later running on x86_64 hardware.

  - macOS 12 (Monterey) and later running on x86_64 hardware.

- Red Hat Enterprise Linux 7 (or equivalent distribution) or later running on one of:

    - x86_64 hardware.
    - AARCH64 hardware.
    - PowerPC (LE) hardware.
    - s390x hardware.

- z/OS version 2.3 on Architecture 11 or later.

Supported platforms in 2025

Altair SLC is supported on the following platforms*:

- *Taken from the installation folder file ../doc/en/WPS-New-in-Release-en.pdf

    - AIX version 7.2 or later running on PowerPC (ppc)/POWER/System p hardware.
    - Microsoft Windows version 10 or later running on x86_64 hardware.
    - Microsoft Windows Server 2016 or later running on x86_64 hardware.
    - macOS 12 (Monterey) and later running on x86_64 hardware.
    - Red Hat Enterprise Linux 8 (or equivalent distribution) or later running on one of:

        - x86_64 hardware.
        - AARCH64 hardware.
        - PowerPC (LE) hardware.
        - s390x hardware.

    - z/OS version 2.3 on Architecture 11 or later.

Altair SLC and the Output Delivery System (ODS)

Altair SLC 5.24 (2024) can send output to a significant proportion of the ODS destinations available in SAS Software. This means that SAS programs using ODS destinations are very likely to have some or all of the features also available in Altair SLC. Currently the ODS destinations included are as follows, remembering that some of the more recently added functionality and options may not exist in Altair SLC yet:

- ODS LISTING
- ODS OLDLISTING (unique to Altair SLC)
- ODS PDF
- ODS RTF
- ODS EXCEL
- ODS POWERPOINT
- ODS PACKAGE
- ODS GRAPHICS
- ODS TEXT
- ODS OUTPUT
- ODS LAYOUT
- ODS REGION
- ODS RESULTS
- ODS TRACE
- ODS MARKUP
    - ODS CHTML is an alias of ODS MARKUP TAGSET=TAGSETS.CHTML
    - ODS CSV is an alias of ODS MARKUP TAGSET=TAGSETS.CSV

- o ODS CSVALL is an alias of ODS MARKUP TAGSET=TAGSETS.CSVALL

- o ODS EXCELXP is an alias of ODS MARKUP TAGSET=TAGSETS.EXCELXP

- o ODS HTML is an alias of ODS MARKUP TAGSET=TAGSETS.HTMLCSS

- o ODS HTMLCSS is an alias of ODS MARKUP TAGSET=TAGSETS.HTMLCSS

- o ODS HTML4 is an alias of ODS MARKUP TAGSET=TAGSETS.HTML4

- o ODS HTML5 is an alias of ODS MARKUP TAGSET=TAGSETS.HTML5

- o ODS MSOFFICE2K is an alias of ODS MARKUP TAGSET=TAGSETS.MSOFFICE2K

- o ODS PHTML is an alias of ODS MARKUP TAGSET=TAGSETS.PHTML

- o ODS XML is an alias of ODS MARKUP TAGSET=TAGSETS.XML

- ODS DOCUMENT and the associated PROC DOCUMENT

ODS DOCUMENT and PROC DOCUMENT example

This sample program is based on a SAS program I published in a conference paper, "Everyday Uses for ODS" at PSI Statistical Computing SIG in 2005. There have been a number of amendments, mostly due to PROC COPY in Altair SLC not being able to select ITEMSTOR (Item Store) member types, so the code writes directly to SASUSER, instead of copying the item store there from WORK:

```
** Create or overwrite an item store **;
ODS DOCUMENT NAME = sasuser.doc1(write);

PROC MEANS DATA = sashelp9.class;
  CLASS age;
  VAR height weight;
RUN;
```

16 What is Altair SLC?

```
PROC TABULATE DATA = sashelp9.class;
  CLASS age;
  VAR height weight;
  TABLE (age ALL)
       ,(height * MEAN weight * MEAN);
RUN;

ODS DOCUMENT CLOSE;

** Producing reports from an Item Store without having to
   re-run your report processing **;
ODS HTML FILE = "ods document.htm" STYLE = Default;

TITLE "All reports";

PROC DOCUMENT;
  DOC;
  DOC NAME = sasuser.doc1;
  LIST / LEVELS = ALL;
  REPLAY;
RUN;
QUIT;
```

This HTML output shows the included items and the selected reports:

All reports

The DOCUMENT Procedure

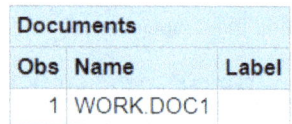

Documents		
Obs	Name	Label
1	WORK.DOC1	

Listing of: \SASUSER.doc1\
Order by: Insertion
Number of levels: ALL

Obs	Path	Type
1	\Means#1	Dir
2	\Means#1\summary#1	Table
3	\Tabulate#1	Dir
4	\Tabulate#1\Tabulate#1	Dir
5	\Tabulate#1\Tabulate#1\Table#1	Table

The MEANS Procedure
Summary statistics

Summary statistics							
Age	N Obs	Variable	N	Mean	Std Dev	Minimum	Maximum
11	2	Height	2	54.400000	4.384062	51.300000	57.500000
		Weight	2	67.750000	24.395184	50.500000	85.000000
12	5	Height	5	59.440000	3.297423	56.300000	64.800000
		Weight	5	94.400000	20.528639	77.000000	128.000000
13	3	Height	3	61.433333	4.495924	56.500000	65.300000
		Weight	3	88.666667	8.082904	84.000000	98.000000
14	4	Height	4	64.900000	2.801190	62.800000	69.000000
		Weight	4	101.875000	9.213893	90.000000	112.500000
15	4	Height	4	65.625000	2.096624	62.500000	67.000000
		Weight	4	117.375000	10.419333	112.000000	133.000000
16	1	Height	1	72.000000	.	72.000000	72.000000
		Weight	1	150.000000	.	150.000000	150.000000

The TABULATE Procedure
Cross-tabular summary report
Table 1

	Height	Weight
	Mean	Mean
Age		
11	54.40	67.75
12	59.44	94.40
13	61.43	88.67
14	64.90	101.88
15	65.63	117.38
16	72.00	150.00
All	62.34	100.03

```
TITLE "Filtered reports";

PROC DOCUMENT;
  DOC;
  DOC NAME = sasuser.doc1;
  DELETE Means#1\Summary#1;
  LIST / LEVELS = ALL;
  REPLAY;
RUN;
QUIT;

ODS HTML CLOSE;
```

This HTML output shows the included items and the selected reports after deleting the MEANS Summary from the item store:

Filtered reports

The DOCUMENT Procedure

Documents		
Obs	Name	Label
1	WORK.DOC1	

Listing of: \SASUSER.doc1
Order by: Insertion
Number of levels: ALL

Obs	Path	Type
1	\Means#1	Dir
2	\Tabulate#1	Dir
3	\Tabulate#1\Tabulate#1	Dir
4	\Tabulate#1\Tabulate#1\Table#1	Table

The TABULATE Procedure
Cross-tabular summary report
Table 1

	Height Mean	Weight Mean
Age		
11	54.40	67.75
12	59.44	94.40
13	61.43	88.67
14	64.90	101.88
15	65.63	117.38
16	72.00	150.00
All	62.34	100.03

Visual Studio Code Editor (VS Code): Altair SLC extension

Instead of using Altair Analytics Workbench to run your SAS programs on local Altair SLC server, you can use a VS Code extension to do it for you.

The Altair SLC extension (currently version 0.7.1) can be set up to access your local Altair SLC installation by adding the following to the **settings.json** file (please edit the following text for your own installation):

```
"slc.connections": [
  {
    "profileName": "slc",
    "type": "local",
    "localInstallDir": "F:/Program Files/Altair/SLC/2024/",
    "autoExec": [{
      "type": "file",
      "filePath": "G:/WPS Workspaces/Altair3/autoexec.sas"
    }],
  }
],
```

Conclusions

If you are looking for a low-cost replacement for SAS Software, then Altair SLC should be considered. However, there are a number of areas where Altair SLC lags a long way behind the current SAS software functionality. This will be discussed further in the subsequent chapters.

Introduction to Altair Analytics Workbench

Introduction

While the fully licensed version of Altair SLC allows users to run SAS programs interactively or in batch, the free Community or Personal Edition includes Altair Analytics Workbench together with the compiler, which runs SAS programs interactively using the Eclipse IDE platform. This chapter looks more closely at the Altair Analytics Workbench, and how it differs from interactive SAS Software, Enterprise Guide and SAS Studio.

When I first started using WPS in 2019 (as Altair Analytics Workbench was called at that time), I had already used the Eclipse IDE platform to develop JavaScript (for webOS and Chrome apps) and Java (for Android apps), so I was fairly familiar with how it could be used.

World Programming and Altair have added to Eclipse's capabilities by adding syntax checking, parsing and running of SAS programs, so that the facilities required by a SAS programmer should be fairly easy to learn. R and Python syntax were already available in Eclipse, so integrating those languages into the platform too was never going to be difficult.

The Altair Analytics Workbench layout and functionality in version 2024 (5.24) has been changed in version 2025 (5.25), so there are separate sections below for each version, but some sub-sections may be repeated where the functionality and appearance remain the same. Please refer to the section corresponding to your installed version.

Analytics Workbench 2024

Supported platforms in 2024

Altair Analytics Workbench 2024 is supported on the following platforms*:

*Taken from **https://help.altair.com/2024/SLC/Altair-SLC-New-in-Release-en.pdf**

- Microsoft Windows version 10 or later running on x86_64 hardware.

- macOS 12 (Monterey) and later running on x86_64 hardware.

- Red Hat Enterprise Linux 7 (or equivalent distribution) or later running on x86_64 hardware.

Initial View

When you open a new installation of Altair Analytics Workbench 2024 you may be asked to specify a Workspace in a window like the one below, but with the suggested folder name determined by the default settings.

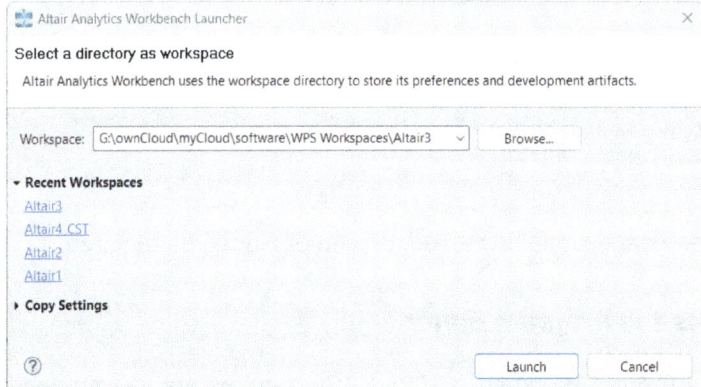

I will explain what a Workspace is used for later in this chapter.

24 Introduction to Altair Analytics Workbench

Having specified the Workspace, the initial view is typical of the Eclipse platform, with panels showing the File Explorer, Text Editor, Results Explorer and Output Explorer.

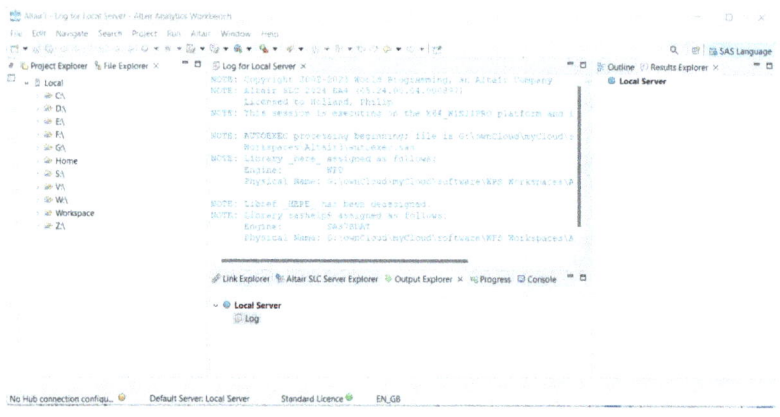

All of these panels can be moved, pinned or hidden as required.

Where is the Program Editor?

In Altair Analytics Workbench 2024 SAS programs are viewed and edited in the Text Editor panel, which uses multi-tab functionality and shows ">>" at the right-hand side if there are more files open than there is space for tabs. The hidden files are then shown in a drop-down menu.

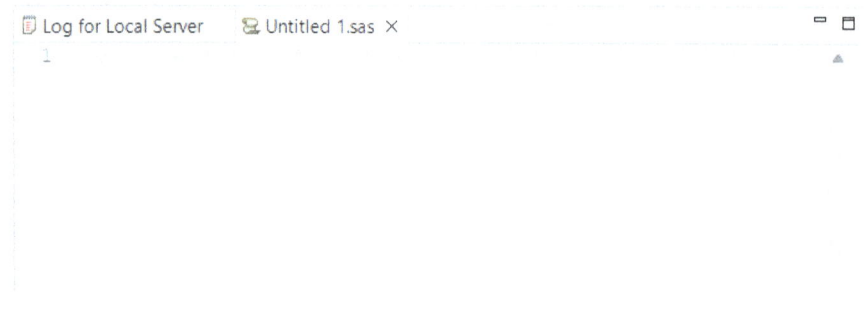

Where is the Log?

Similar to the Project Log in SAS Enterprise Guide and the Log window in an interactive SAS session, the Log for Local Server contains all of the Log information since either the Local Server was started, or the Log for Local Server was last cleared.

```
Log for Local Server  X   Untitled 1.sas
NOTE: Copyright 2002-2023 World Programming, an Altair Company
NOTE: Altair SLC 2024 EA4 (05.24.00.04.000897)
      Licensed to Holland, Philip
NOTE: This session is executing on the X64_WIN11PRO platform and i
NOTE: AUTOEXEC processing beginning; file is G:\ownCloud\myCloud\s
      Workspaces\Altair3\autoexec.sas
NOTE: Library _here_ assigned as follows:
      Engine:          WPD
      Physical Name: G:\ownCloud\myCloud\software\WPS Workspaces\A
NOTE: Libref _HERE_ has been deassigned.
NOTE: Library sashelp9 assigned as follows:
      Engine:          SAS7BDAT
      Physical Name: G:\ownCloud\myCloud\software\WPS Workspaces\A
NOTE: AUTOEXEC processing completed
```

Where is my Output?

Output can be found by ODS destination in the Output Explorer,

or by program step in the Results Explorer.

26   Introduction to Altair Analytics Workbench

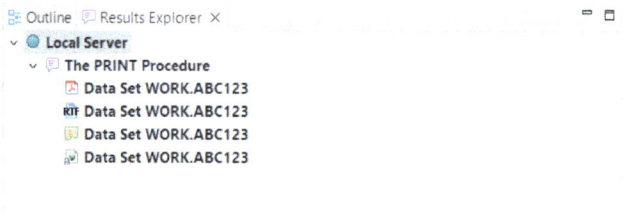

Double-clicking on each output will open it in its associated viewer.

Where are the Libraries and File References?

Libraries, whether they contain SAS data sets (SAS7BDAT, V8, or V9; SD2 or V6) or Altair SLC data sets (WPD, which is the default library engine), and file references (Filerefs) can be found under the Altair SLC Server Explorer tab. Clicking on Libraries will expand the hierarchy to show the data sets, and clicking on the data set names will expand the hierarchy again to show their variables.

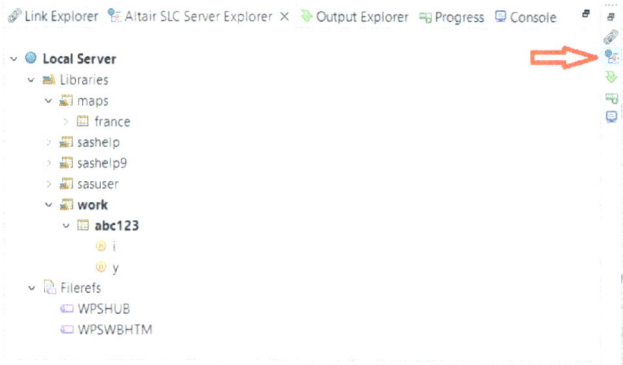

Double-clicking a data set name will open that data set in a Data Viewer tab next to the Text Editor tabs.

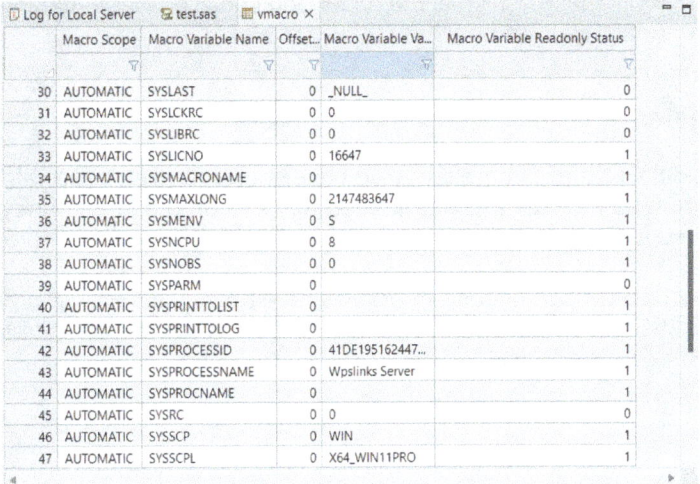

File Explorer

The File Explorer panel includes all of your mapped drives, with 2 special locations:

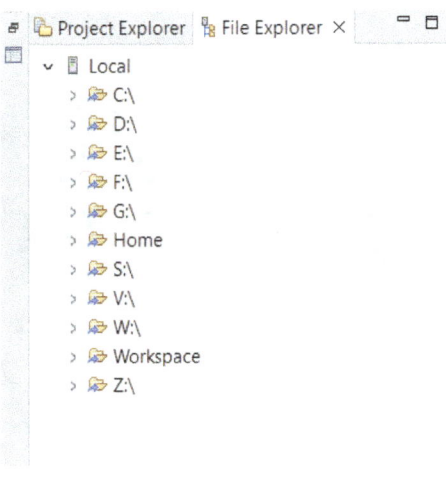

- Home: where your personal folders (Documents, Downloads, Pictures, etc.) can be found.

- Workspace: which is the folder you specified when starting Altair Analytics Workbench 2024.

Project Explorer

The Project Explorer is an alternative file explorer for files associated with a project, but, as projects are not needed for SAS programming, they will not be covered further here.

Workbench users can choose to organise their files into Eclipse projects via the Project Explorer panel, or to simply follow the usual folder/file structure via the File Explorer panel.

Help

Clicking [Help] on the main menu will drop down the Help menu.

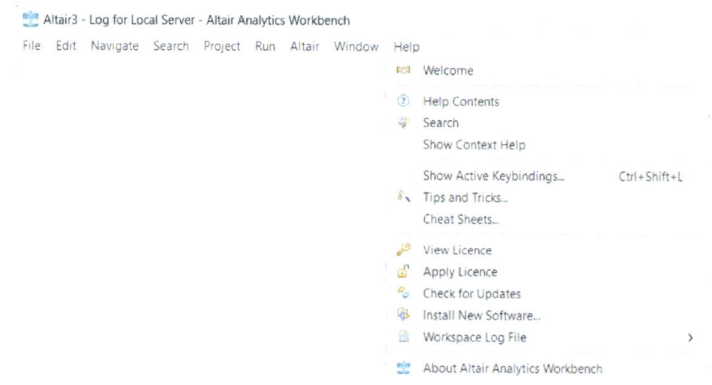

Clicking on the [Help Contents] item on the drop-down menu will display the following window.

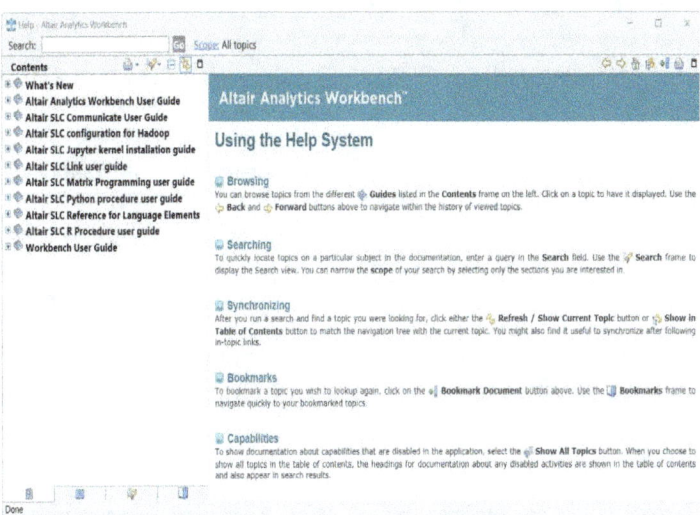

Typing a SAS programming keyword into the Search field and clicking [Go] will display a list of relevant help entries, and clicking on one of the entries will display the text in the right-hand panel.

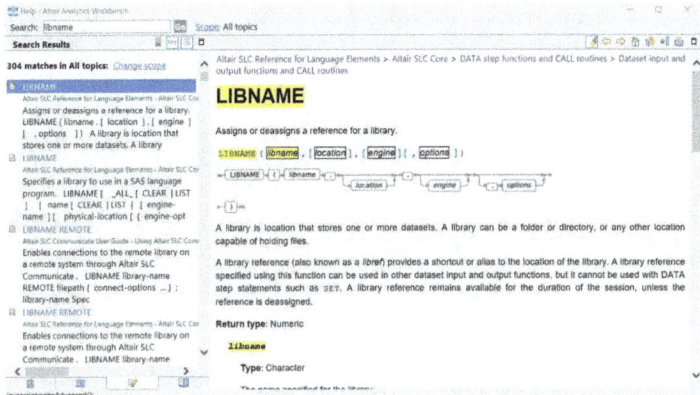

Analytics Workbench 2025

Supported platforms in 2025

Altair Analytics Workbench 2025 is supported on the following platforms*:

*Taken from the installation folder,file ../doc/en/WPS-New-in-Release-en.pdf

- Microsoft Windows version 10 or later running on x86_64 hardware.
- macOS 12 (Monterey) and later running on x86_64 hardware.
- Red Hat Enterprise Linux 8 (or equivalent distribution) or later running on x86_64 hardware.

Initial View

When you open a new installation of Altair Analytics Workbench 2025 you may be asked to specify a Workspace in a window like the one below, but with the suggested folder name determined by the default settings.

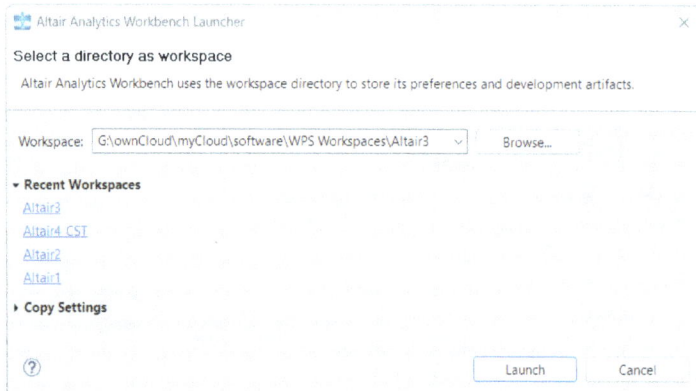

I will explain what a Workspace is used for later in this chapter.

Having specified the Workspace, the initial view is typical of the Eclipse platform, with panels showing the File Explorer, Text Editor, SLC Servers and Outputs.

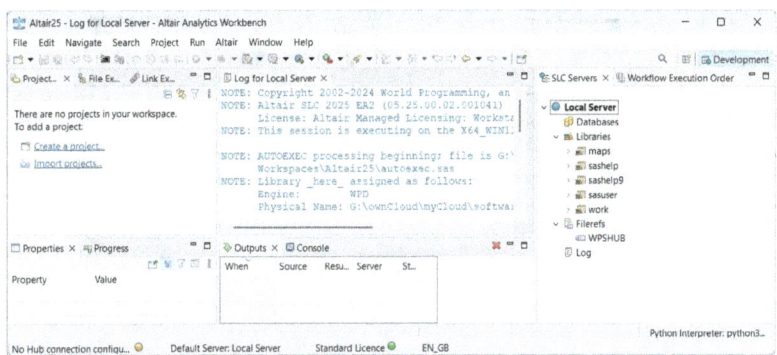

All of these panels can be moved, pinned or hidden as required.

Where is the Program Editor?

In Altair Analytics Workbench 2025 SAS programs are viewed and edited in the Text Editor panel, which uses multi-tab functionality and shows ">>" at the right-hand side if there are more files open than there is space for tabs. The hidden files are then shown in a drop-down menu.

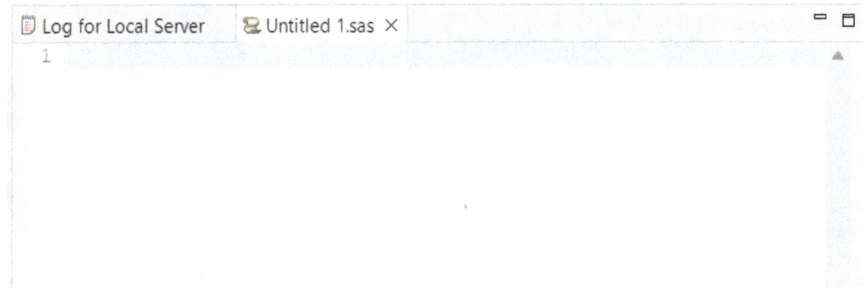

Where is the Log?

Similar to the Project Log in SAS Enterprise Guide and the Log window in an interactive SAS session, the Log for Local Server contains all of the Log information since either the Local Server was started, or the Log for Local Server was last cleared.

Where is my Output?

Output can be found by ODS destination in the Outputs tab,

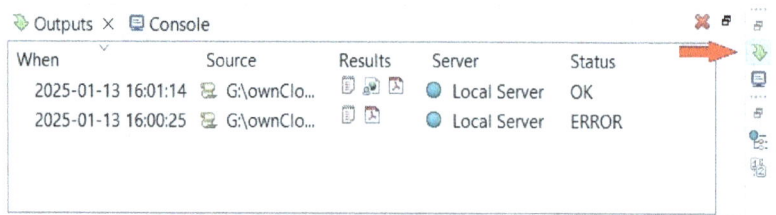

Double-clicking on each output will open it in its associated viewer.

Where are the Libraries and File References?

Libraries, whether they contain SAS data sets (SAS7BDAT, V8, or V9; SD2 or V6) or Altair SLC data sets (WPD, which is the default library engine), and file references (Filerefs) can be found under the SLC Servers tab. Clicking on Libraries will expand the hierarchy to show the data sets, and clicking on the data set names will expand the hierarchy again to show their variables.

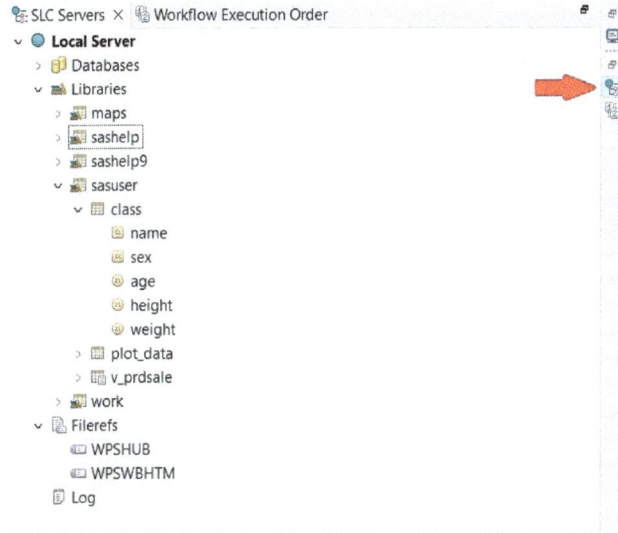

34 Introduction to Altair Analytics Workbench

Double-clicking a data set name will open that data set in a Data Viewer tab next to the Text Editor tabs.

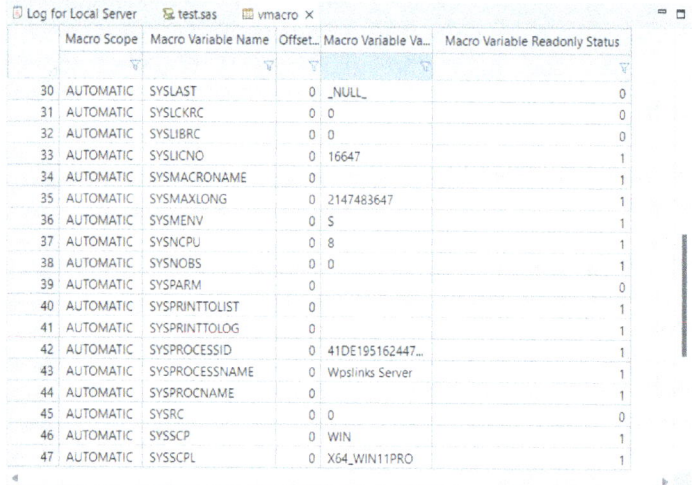

File Explorer

The File Explorer panel includes all of your mapped drives, with 2 special locations:

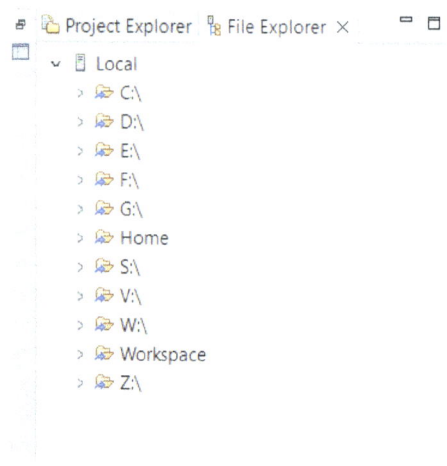

- Home: where your personal folders (Documents, Downloads, Pictures, etc.) can be found.

- Workspace: which is the folder you specified when starting Altair Analytics Workbench 2025.

Project Explorer

The Project Explorer is an alternative file explorer for files associated with a project, but, as projects are not needed for SAS programming, they will not be covered further here.

Workbench users can choose to organise their files into Eclipse projects via the Project Explorer panel, or to simply follow the usual folder/file structure via the File Explorer panel.

Help

Clicking [Help] on the main menu will drop down the Help menu.

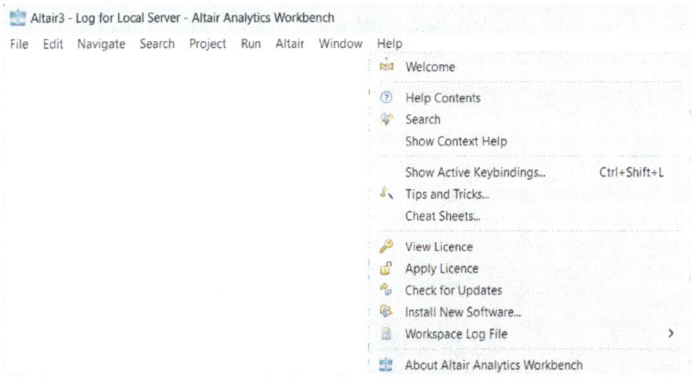

36 Introduction to Altair Analytics Workbench

Clicking on the [Help Contents] item on the drop-down menu will display the following window.

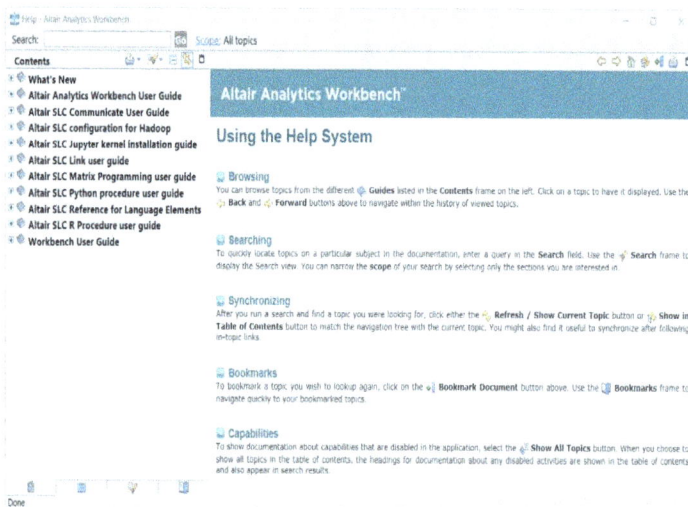

Typing a SAS programming keyword into the Search field and clicking [Go] will display a list of relevant help entries, and clicking on one of the entries will display the text in the right-hand panel.

Differences from Interactive SAS, Enterprise Guide and SAS Studio

What is a Workspace?

Altair Analytics Workbench runs on an Eclipse platform, which uses a Workspace folder to store plug-in information and platform settings. Altair Analytics Workbench can use the same folder as a default location for storing programs, data and other files.

The Workspace can be switched from the File menu:

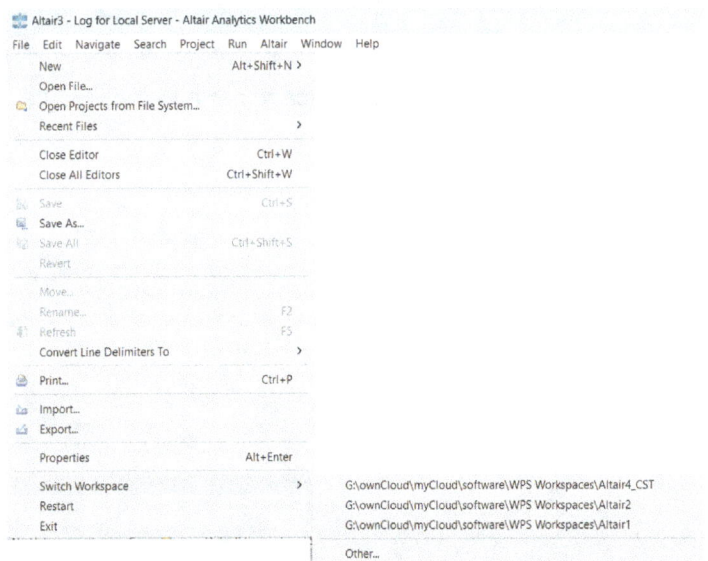

38 Introduction to Altair Analytics Workbench

Clicking on [Other...] will display the following window, so you can specify a new workspace folder, or select a recent workspace.

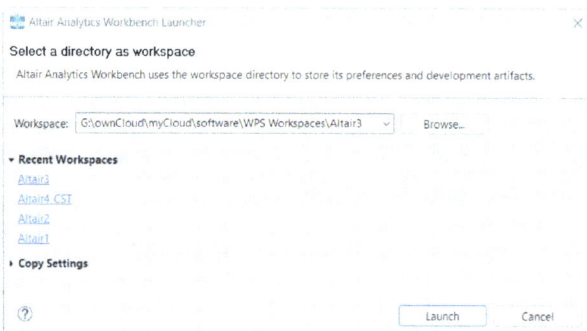

Please note that selecting a new workspace folder and clicking [Launch] will cause the session to restart.

Setting the Current Working Folder

By default the current working folder will be the same as the Workspace being used by Eclipse for Altair Analytics Workbench. However, this behaviour can be changed to match the folder containing the program being run. Click [Preferences] in the drop-down menu under [Window], and select the [Code Submission] tab. The [Set working directory to program directory on code submission] checkbox will change the current working folder each time a program is run.

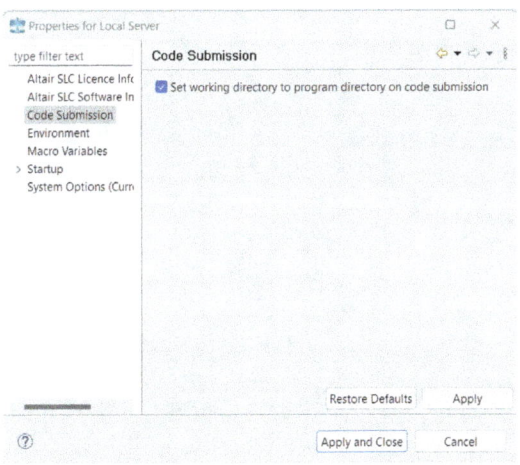

Associating File Types

Associated software, both internal to Altair Analytics Workbench or external programs like a web browser, can be assigned to file types using the [Content Types] tab under [Preferences]

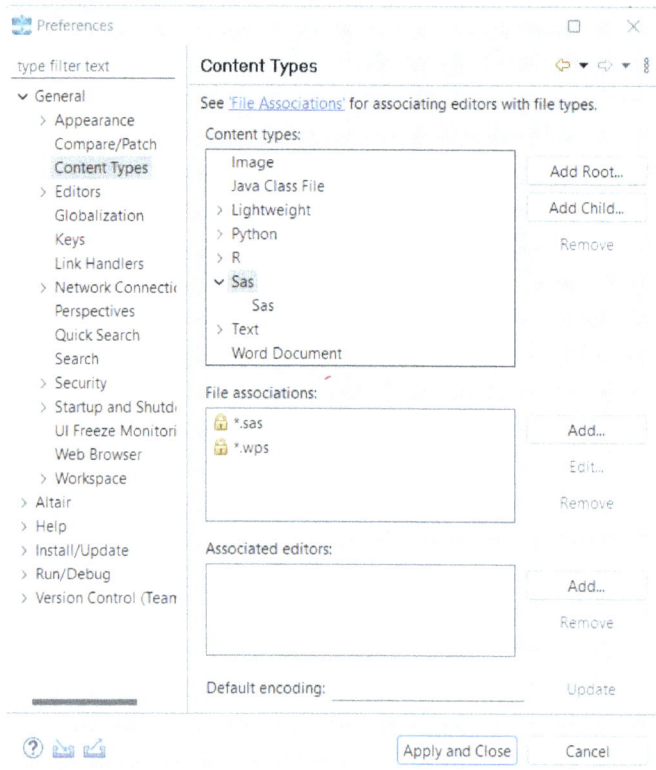

or using [File Association] tab under [Preferences] > [Editor], which will override the Content Type:

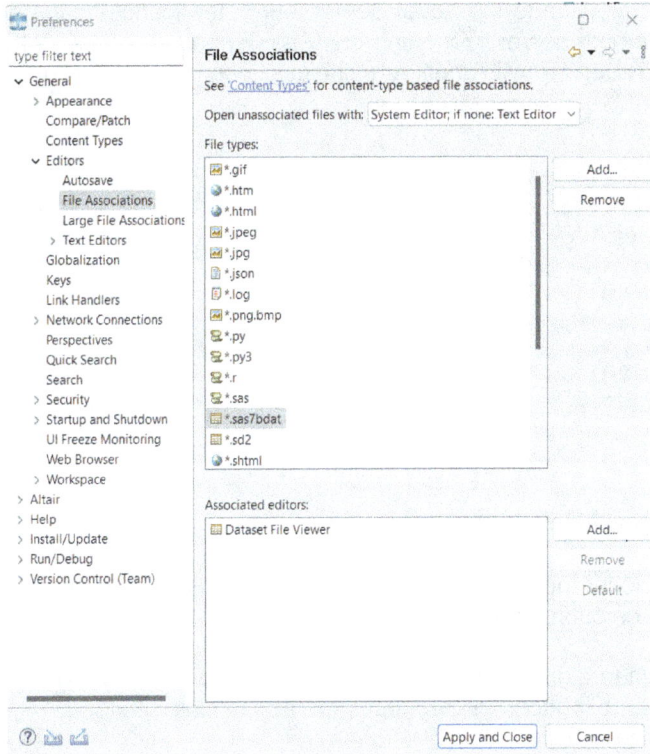

Assigning an Altair SLC Server

The Community or Personal Edition of Altair Analytics Workbench only permits connection to the Local Server, but other licences can connect to a range of remote servers. Opening the [Altair] menu and clicking [Set Default Altair SLC Server] will offer you choices when using the other licences available.

Running SAS Programs

Taking a closer look at a program in the Text Editor, there are several ways that it can be submitted to run on a server:

- When a program is open in the Text Editor it can be run using the [Run] button in the toolbar above the editor.

Altair SLC **43**

- Right-clicking on a program opens a pop-up menu, where clicking the [Run] item will also run the program.

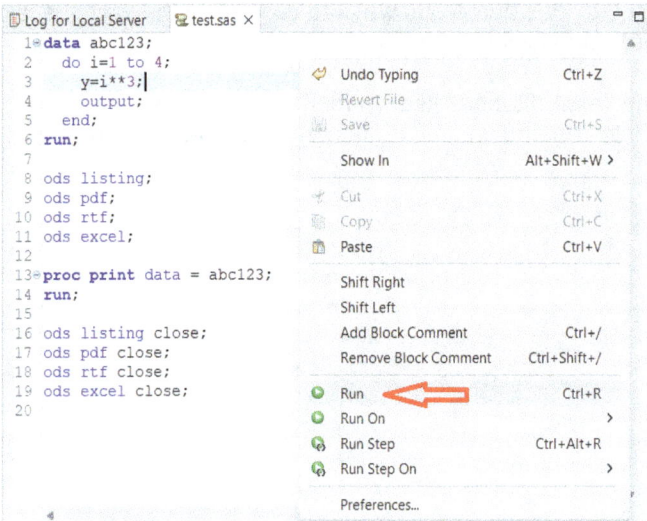

- Opening the [Altair] menu and clicking [Run File......] in the drop-down menu

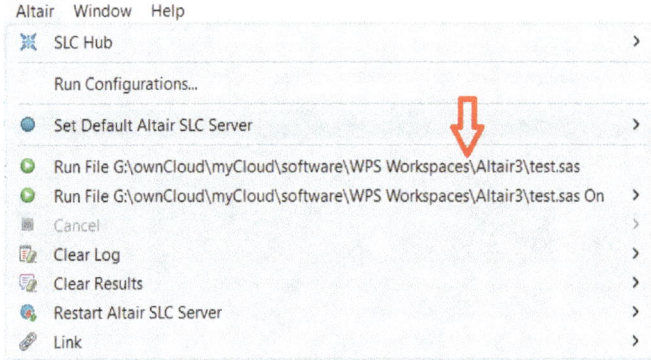

Customising Workbench

Every programmer has their own way of working, so Altair Analytics Workbench provides numerous ways to customise the way it is laid out, and which panels are visible at any time:

- The Text Editor has its own menu to change settings using the [Editor] menu in the [Window] drop-down menu.

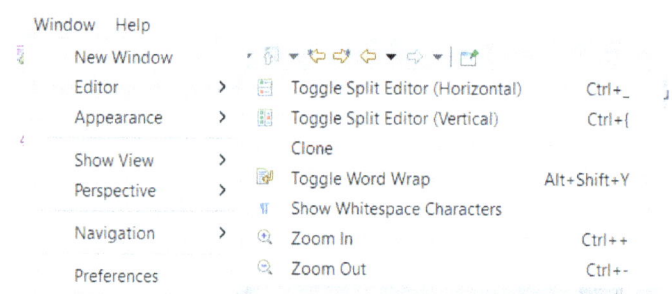

- The screen layout has its own menu to change settings using the [Appearance] menu in the [Window] drop-down menu.

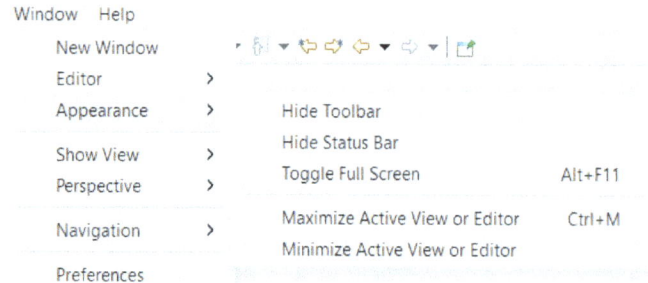

- The panels that may have been hidden can be made visible again using the [Show View] menu in the [Window] drop-down menu in Altair Analytics Workbench 2024

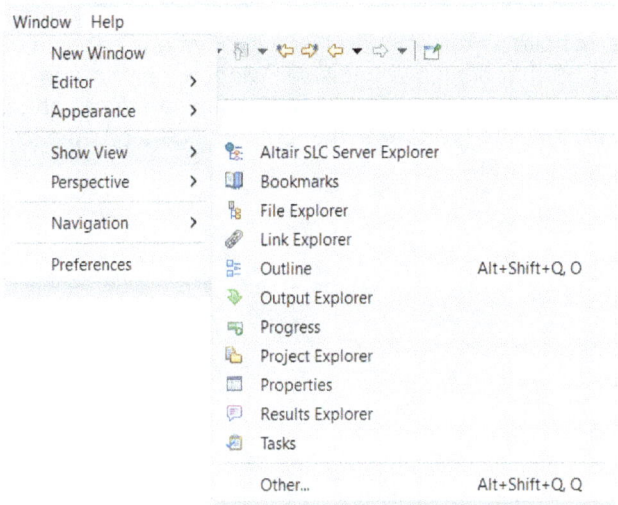

- or in Altair Analytics Workbench 2025.

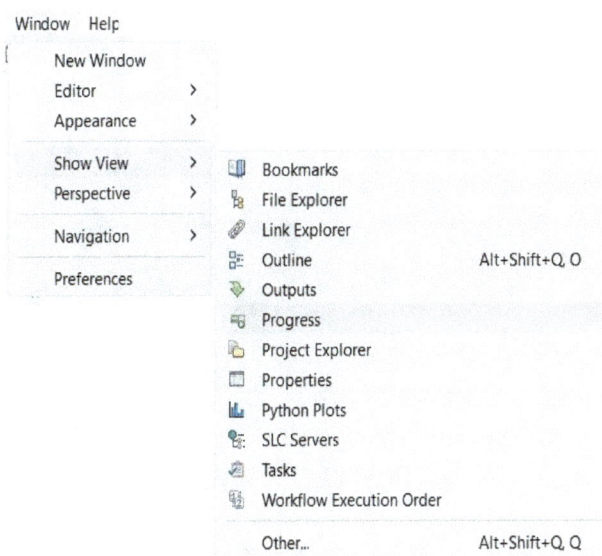

Conclusions

While the screen layout is based around Eclipse, SAS programmers will not find it too difficult to navigate around Altair Analytics Workbench, because the familiar SAS Software windows for the Editor, Log, Output and Libraries all exist and behave as expected. If I was to have any criticism of the layout, then it would be that finding a particular window can be non-trivial, as it is unnervingly easy to move, maximise and minimise them. Fortunately, when you lose a window, the [Windows] menu item should be able to find it again for you.

Altair SLC for Clinical Trials

Introduction

SAS software licences historically included the SAS Clinical Standards Toolkit (CST) as an optional free component. Since July 2022 though, this component has been removed from the licence, and moved to GitHub, as a freely available open-source resource (which can be found at **https://github.com/sassoftware/clinical-standards-toolkit**) for all SAS programmers to develop data processing for clinical trials. The sample SAS programs and data are actually intended to demonstrate the functionality of the toolkit to generate DefineXML, which is a file central to regulatory oversight of clinical trials.

As the toolkit is based on freely available SAS programs, it seemed reasonable to use it as a data source to test whether Altair SLC could be used to process Clinical Trials data.

As soon as I started using the CST sample data I realised that this version of the sample SDTM data had never been used to create the sample ADaM data, so I used Altair SLC to rebuild the necessary metadata, and then generated a consistent set of SDTM and ADaM data. This can now be found at my fork of the CST, which contains only the sample data with most of the unnecessary files from the original CST project removed (found at **https://github.com/hollandnumerics/clinical-standards-data**).

Chapter Glossary

- **Fork**
  This is a term used in open-source software development. A fork is a copy of an existing open-source application or database, which has then been updated. LibreOffice was a fork of OpenOffice.org, when Oracle took over its maintenance, and then made no immediate updates.

- **CDISC** (Clinical Data Interchange Standards Consortium)
  The Clinical Data Interchange Standards Consortium is a standards-developing organization dealing with medical research data for healthcare, to enable information system interoperability to improve medical research and related areas of healthcare.

  - **SDTM** (Study Data Tabulation Model)
    Part of the CDISC standards, the Study Data Tabulation Model (SDTM) defines a standard structure for human clinical trial (study) data tabulations and for non-clinical study data tabulations, that are to be submitted as part of a product application, to a regulatory authority such as the United States Food and Drug Administration (FDA).

48 Altair SLC for Clinical Trials

- **ADaM** (Analysis Data Model)
  Part of the CDISC standards, the Analysis Data Model (ADaM) specifies principles for analysis datasets and standards for a subject-level analysis file and for a basic data structure, which can be used for a wide variety of analysis methods.

The Rules of Clinical Trials Programming

Note that there is no way I can force you to use Altair SLC, SAS OnDemand for Academics, or fully licensed SAS software to complete any of the following programming tasks. However, whichever programming environment you work in, the rules of clinical trials programming will be as follows:

- The production SAS programs may be readable, but should never be copied, either in part or in full.

- The programming logic is determined solely by the metadata. If the metadata is unclear, then you should contact the metadata developer for clarification.

- Program logs can never include ERROR, WARNING or variable uninitialised NOTE messages.

- Hard-coded locations can only be used in **autoexec.sas**, and not in any other programs.

- The final generated SAS data set, when compared to the sample ADaM data set must match within reasonable limits. Note that Data Steps and PROC SQL steps can generate slightly different results, due to differences in the way calculations are evaluated, but these differences should always be within 0.001%.

Configuring Altair SLC

This configuration amendment only updates **autoexec.sas**, so it applies equally to Altair SLC and SAS software.

1. Download the data from **https://github.com/hollandnumerics/clinical-standards-data**. This can either be done by downloading and extracting the zip file from the web page, or by using GitHub to create a clone of the repository, onto your PC.

2. Make a note of the location of the local folders under **clinical-standards-data\standards**.

Altair SLC **49**

3. Create a new folder under your default directory called **adamdata**, which will be used to store your own versions of the ADaM data sets.

4. Create a new file called **autoexec.sas** in your default folder.

5. Assign the following libraries in **autoexec.sas**:

    o **METADATA** - pointing to **cstadam21\source\sample\sascstdemodata\metadata** (CDISC ADaM 2.1) under the repository standards folder. This should be assigned with **ACCESS=READONLY**. This will be used to assign variable lengths and labels in the new ADaM data sets.

    o **SDTM** - pointing to **cstsdtm32\source\sample\ sascstdemodata\data** (CDISC SDTM 3.2) under the repository standards folder. This should be assigned with **ACCESS=READONLY**. This will be where the SDTM data sets will be read for the new ADaM data sets.

    o **ADAM_CST** - pointing to **cstadam21\source\sample\sascstdemodata\data** (CDISC ADaM 2.1) under the repository standards folder. This should be assigned with **ACCESS=READONLY**. This will be where the production ADaM data sets will be read for comparison with the new ADaM data sets.

    o **ADAM** - pointing to the **adamdata** folder in your default directory, where your new ADaM data sets will be stored. Make sure that in Altair SLC that this library uses an engine of V9 or SAS7BDAT to create ***.sas7bdat** files. The default engine for a library pointing to an empty folder in Altair SLC is WPD to create ***.wpd** files, which SAS users will not be able to read! Libraries pointing to a populated folder will use the engine appropriate to the files already present.

6. Submit **autoexec.sas** to assign the libraries. This will be done automatically when you restart your Altair SLC or SAS session.

Useful Input Data Sets

Before starting any SAS programming, it is very important that you have thoroughly read the programming information stored in the following variables in **metadata.source_columns**:

- ORIGIN. This contains one of the following values:

    o "Predecessor", which means that this variable is a copy of an existing variable in another data set. See ORIGINDESCRIPTION for details.

- "Assigned", which means that a fixed value will be stored in this variable. See ALGORITHM for details.

- "Derived", which means that this value is calculated. See ALGORITHM for details.

- ORIGINDESCRIPTION. This contains the name of the existing variable to copy.

- ALGORITHM. This contains the algorithm to be used to calculate the value.

The following variables in **metadata.source_tables** can be used to update the final ADaM data sets:

- TABLE. The name of the ADaM data set.

- LABEL. The label of the ADaM data set.

- KEYS. The sort order of the ADaM data set separated by spaces.

The following variables in **metadata.source_columns** can be used to generate ATTRIB statements to specify the variable attributes in the final ADaM data sets:

- TABLE. The name of the ADaM data set.

- NAME. The name of the variable.

- LABEL. The label of the variable.

- TYPE. The type of variable: 'C' (character) or 'N' (numeric).

- LENGTH. The length of the variable, which is only relevant if TYPE='C'.

- FORMAT: The display format of the variable, if non-missing.

Macro to Standardise and Compare ADaM Data Sets

This macro will do the following:

- Extract the variable lengths, labels and formats from metadata.source_columns.

- Extract the data set label and sort order from metadata.source_tables.

- Apply the extracted metadata to standardise the ADaM data set.

Altair SLC **51**

- Sort the ADaM data set using the key variables.

```
%MACRO use_metadata(indsn=, outdsn=, table=, debug=N);
* Create a catalog source member to store the programs *;
FILENAME src CATALOG "work.meta_&table.";

** Extract the variable metadata from source_columns **;
DATA _NULL_;
  SET metadata.source_columns;
  WHERE table = "%upcase(&table.)";
  LENGTH _label _format _length $200;
  FILE src(columns.source);
  IF _N_ = 1 THEN PUT "KEEP=" column;
  ELSE PUT " " column;
  FILE src(attrib.source);
  _label = STRIP(label);
  _format = STRIP(displayformat);
  _length = STRIP(PUT(length, 8.));
  PUT "ATTRIB " column;
  IF CMISS(_label) = 0 THEN
    PUT " LABEL='" _label +(-1) "'";
  IF CMISS(_format) = 0 THEN PUT " FORMAT=" _format;
  IF type = "C" AND NMISS(length) = 0 THEN
    PUT " LENGTH=$" _length;
  PUT " ;";
  FILE src(initial.source);
  PUT column "= " column ";";
RUN;

** Extract the data set metadata from source_tables **;
DATA _NULL_;
  SET metadata.source_tables;
  WHERE table = "%upcase(&table.)";
  LENGTH _label $200;
  FILE src(dslabel.source);
  _label = STRIP(label);
  PUT " (LABEL='" _label +(-1) "');";
  FILE src(sort.source);
  PUT keys ";";
RUN;

** Update the input data set with the metadata **;
DATA &indsn._a (
  %INCLUDE src(columns.source);
          );
  %INCLUDE src(attrib.source);
  SET &indsn.;
  %INCLUDE src(initial.source);
RUN;

** Create the ADaM data set with the correct sorting **;
PROC SORT DATA = &indsn._a
          OUT = &outdsn.
  %INCLUDE src(dslabel.source);;
  BY %INCLUDE src(sort.source);
RUN;
```

```
** Compare with &table in ADAM_CST **;
PROC COMPARE BASE = adam_cst.&table. COMPARE = &outdsn.
            LISTALL BRIEFSUMMARY MAXPRINT = (5000, 100)
            METHOD = RELATIVE CRITERION = 0.001;
    ID %INCLUDE src(sort.source);
RUN;

** Delete temporary data sets, if not debugging **;
%if %upcase(&debug.) NE N %then %do;
  PROC DATASETS;
    DELETE &indsn._a;
  RUN;
  QUIT;
%end;
%MEND use_metadata;
```

Store this macro in the same folder as the ADaM program, or in a folder that is part of the SASAUTOS list, so that it can be called without including the program first.

To call **%use_metadata** use the following sample code with your own input and output data sets for each table:

```
%use_metadata(indsn=adqs1, outdsn=adam.adqs, table=adqs);
```

Remember to assign the **metadata** and **adam_cst** library references to the folders from the downloaded GitHub repository before running the macro. See the "Configuring Altair SLC" section above for more details.

Over to You!

Now you have all of the information available to a biostatistical SAS programmer, can you use all of the data sets and metadata listed above to re-create the SAS data sets in your **ADAM** library that match those in my **ADAM_CST** library?

- ADSL - Subject-level data (CDISC ADSL data) - 70 records and 25 variables.

- ADAE - Adverse Event data (CDISC OCCDS data) - 106 records and 61 variables.

- ADQS - Questionnaire data (CDISC BDS data) - 14857 records and 24 variables.

- ADTTE - Time-to-Event data (CDISC BDS data) - 70 records and 15 variables.

Altair SLC **53**

How Did You Get On?

What you have been doing is called Quality Control (QC) of the ADaM data sets. It is vital that the QC is completely independent of the production programs, although using certain validated macros would be accepted. Therefore, if you can answer 'Yes' to all of the following questions for all of the 4 ADaM data sets, then your QC has been successful, and you will be asked to sign off the production programs:

- Does the ADaM data set in the **ADAM_CST** library match your data set in the **ADAM** library within the matching criteria?

- Is your program log free of ERROR and WARNING messages?

- Is your program log free of uninitialised variable NOTE messages?

- No OPTIONS statement to suppress messages has been used in your program?

- No hard-coded locations have been used in %INCLUDE, FILENAME, LIBNAME and FILE statements? All hard-coded locations should only appear in **autoexec.sas**.

If you have answered any of these questions with a 'No', you will need to update your programs to correct them, just like a typical QC programmer on a Clinical Trail.

Conclusions

- Clinical trials data processing uses a limited subset of SAS programming syntax, and Altair SLC (WPS) was designed to cover the vast majority of this subset.

- When creating the production SAS programs (using Altair SLC), I used a wide range of Data Step statements, Base SAS procedures, dictionary views and PROC SQL to test the compatibility with SAS Software.

- If you remembered that the WPS Workspace assigned to the Altair Analytics Workbench is the default folder (and cannot be changed!), then all of the file locations should be relative to this folder.

- The **autoexec.sas** updates are the key to a successful SAS programming environment in Altair SLC.

Generating Graphics with Altair SLC

Introduction

When creating graphs with SAS programs in Altair SLC, almost all of the program statements from SAS/GRAPH and ODS Graphics can be utilised. This chapter takes programming examples from my previous graphics books and published papers to test the graphics capabilities of Altair SLC.

In the following examples the library SASHELP9 points to the SASHELP folders installed in SAS 9.4, which include the CLASS and PRDSAL2 data sets. Altair SLC includes its own SASHELP library, so the SASHELP9 library reference is used to identify the SAS-supplied version. If needed, an alternative copy of the data sets from the SAS version of the SASHELP library, can be downloaded from https://hollandnumerics.org.uk/wordpress/sashelp/

Apart from changing **sashelp.class** to **sashelp9.class**, the same SAS code that worked in SAS 9.4 is being used, unless otherwise stated.

How Many Ways to Create Graphs?

SAS/GRAPH

The traditional graphs created with SAS programs used a component called SAS/GRAPH. Many of the SAS/GRAPH procedures are available in Altair SLC too, although not all features have been included to date. These SAS/GRAPH procedures are:

- PROC GPLOT
- PROC GCHART
- PROC GMAP
- PROC GSLIDE
- PROC GCONTOUR
- PROC G3GRID

- PROC GANNO

- PROC GREPLAY

Examples using PROC GPLOT and PROC GCHART have been included later in this chapter.

Note, however, that DSGI functions, part of SAS/GRAPH, have not been included in Altair SLC.

ODS Graphics 'SG' Procedures

Introduced from SAS 9.2, the ODS Graphics procedures are now becoming available in Altair SLC, but, again, with reduced functionality. These ODS Graphics procedures are:

- PROC SGPLOT

- PROC SGPANEL

- PROC SGSCATTER

- PROC SGPIE

Examples using PROC SGPLOT and PROC SGPIE have been included later in this chapter.

ODS Graphics with Graph Templates

A pre-production release of ODS Graph Templates was included in SAS 9.1.3, but was changed significantly in the production release in SAS 9.2.

In SAS 9.1.3 and later releases the STATGRAPH templates created in PROC TEMPLATE could be rendered in DATA _NULL_ steps using the FILE PRINT ODS=() and PUT _ODS_ statements, but this feature only works with TABLE templates in Altair SLC.

From SAS version 9.2 the PROC SGRENDER step can be used to render the templates, but can only be used in Altair SLC with limitations, as this procedure is still Experimental in version 5.23 (2023), but is Production in version 5.24 (2024).

Scatter Plots

In Altair SLC, scatter plots using PROC GPLOT and PROC SGPLOT are very similar to those created using SAS, except that the x-axis ranges are the same for both procedures (unlike in SAS software!), and like PROC SGPLOT. This is a vast improvement! Although the y-axis ranges are different for reasons unknown.

The Altair SLC code only differs from the SAS/GRAPH code by using the SASHELP9 library reference, which refers to the SAS 9.4 installation libraries. By default, Altair SLC has its own SASHELP library reference, which refers to its own system data sets.

PROC GPLOT

```
PROC GPLOT DATA = sashelp9.class;
    SYMBOL V = CIRCLE I = NONE;
    PLOT weight * height = sex;
RUN;
```

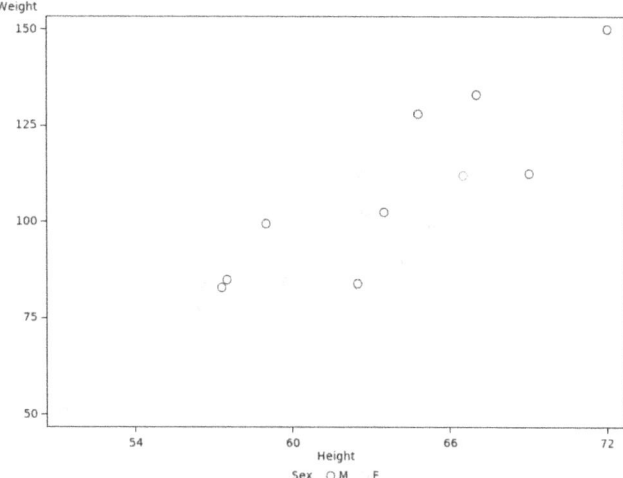

PROC SGPLOT

```
PROC SGPLOT DATA = sashelp9.class;
    SCATTER Y = weight X = height
            / GROUP = sex;
RUN;
```

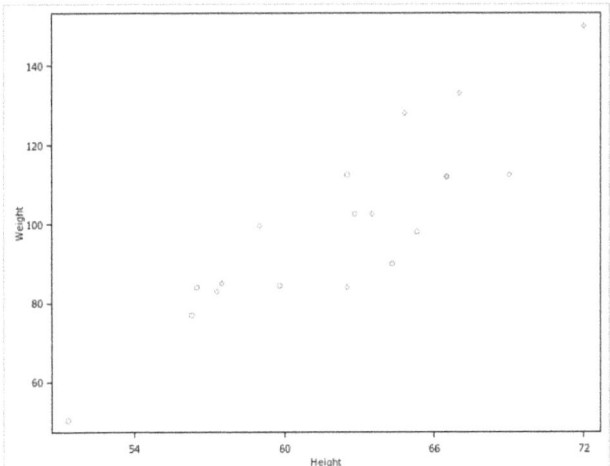

Line Plots

In Altair SLC, line plots using PROC GPLOT and PROC SGPLOT are very similar to those created using SAS, except that the x-axis ranges are the same for both procedures (unlike in SAS software!), and like PROC SGPLOT. This is a vast improvement! Although the y-axis tick marks are different for reasons unknown.

The Altair SLC code only differs from the SAS/GRAPH code by using the SASHELP9 library reference, which refers to the SAS 9.4 installation libraries. By default, Altair SLC has a SASHELP library reference, which refers to its own system data sets.

PROC GPLOT

```
PROC SORT DATA = sashelp9.class
          OUT = class;
    BY sex height;
RUN;
```

```
PROC GPLOT DATA = class;
   SYMBOL V = CIRCLE I = JOIN;
   PLOT weight * height = sex;
RUN;
```

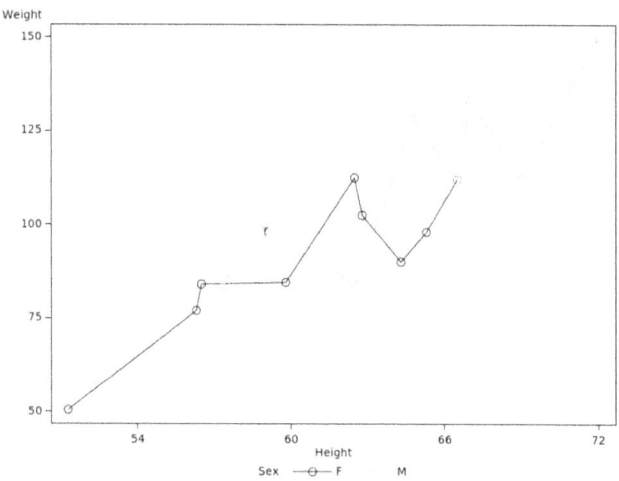

PROC SGPLOT

```
PROC SORT DATA = sashelp9.class
          OUT = class;
   BY sex height;
RUN;

PROC SGPLOT DATA = class;
   SERIES Y = weight X = height
          / GROUP = sex MARKERS
            MARKERATTRS = (SYMBOL=CIRCLE);
RUN;
```

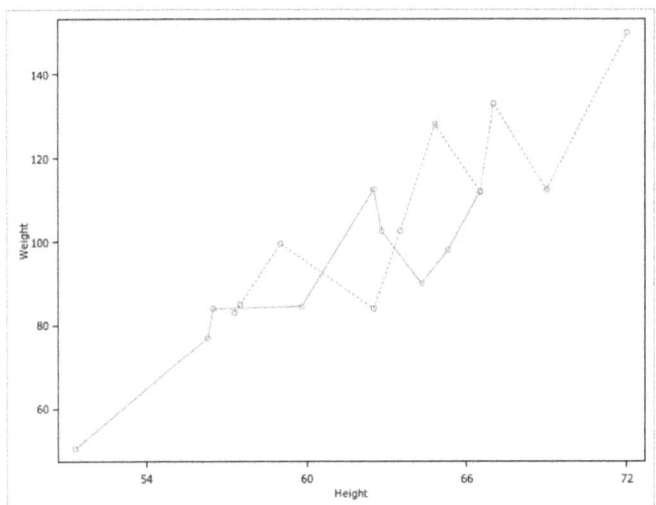

Regression Plots

Regression plots can be created in Altair SLC using PROC GPLOT and PROC SGPLOT, but lines showing the confidence limits are only generated in PROC SGPLOT. However, in Altair SLC, the x-axis ranges are the same for both procedures (unlike in SAS software!), and like PROC SGPLOT. This is a vast improvement! Although the y-axis tick marks are different for reasons unknown.

The Altair SLC code only differs from the SAS/GRAPH code by using the SASHELP9 library reference, which refers to the SAS 9.4 installation libraries. By default, Altair SLC has a SASHELP library reference, which refers to its own system data sets.

PROC GPLOT

In the following program R0CLI95 has been commented out, because the SYMBOL statement in Altair SLC only includes the following values for I= (INTERPOL=): NONE, JOIN, NEEDLE, SPLINE, STEP or R. Therefore the regression plot is only drawn with the regression line using I=R, and without the confidence limits.

60 Generating Graphics with Altair SLC

The regression lines are only extended to the range of that group of data points.

```
PROC SORT DATA = sashelp9.class
          OUT = class;
     BY sex height;
RUN;

PROC GPLOT DATA = class;
     SYMBOL V = CIRCLE I = R /*R0CLI95*/;
     PLOT weight * height = sex;
RUN;
```

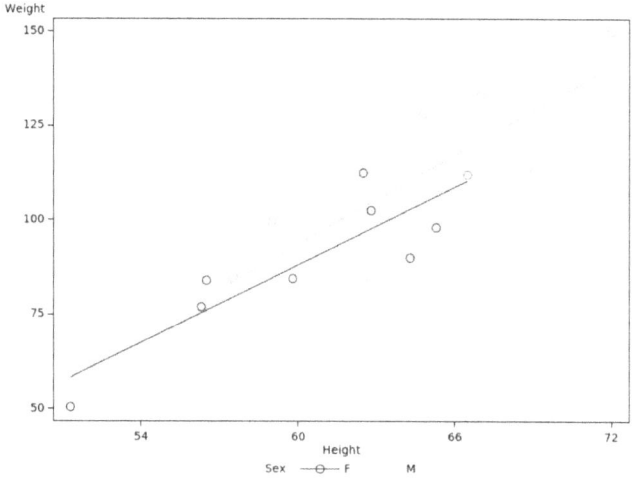

PROC SGPLOT

Confidence Interval lines are added when the regression plot is created by PROC SGPLOT, and the confidence and regression lines are extrapolated to the range of the entire data set.

```
PROC SORT DATA = sashelp9.class
          OUT = class;
     BY sex height;
RUN;
```

```
PROC SGPLOT DATA = class;
    REG Y = weight X = height
        / GROUP = sex CLI
          MARKERATTRS = (SYMBOL=CIRCLE);
RUN;
```

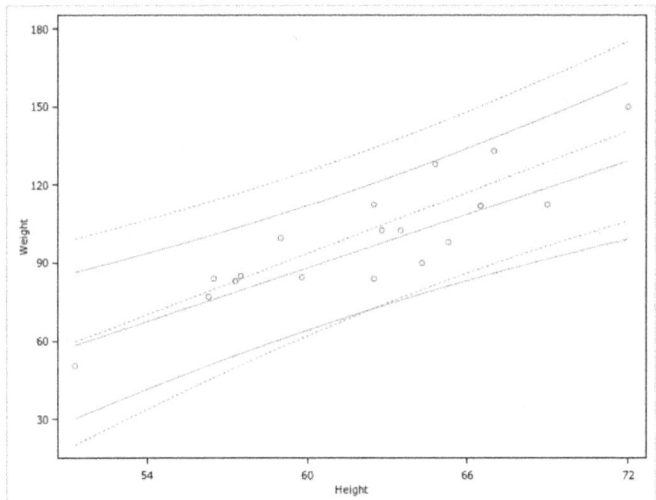

Error Bar Plots

In Altair SLC, error bar plots using PROC GPLOT and PROC SGPLOT are very similar to those created using SAS, except that the x-axis ranges are the same for both procedures (unlike in SAS software!), and like PROC SGPLOT. This is a vast improvement! Although the y-axis tick marks are different for reasons unknown.

The Altair SLC code only differs from the SAS/GRAPH code by using the SASHELP9 library reference, which refers to the SAS 9.4 installation libraries. By default, Altair SLC has a SASHELP library reference, which refers to its own system data sets.

PROC GPLOT

Standard SAS programs generating line plots with error bars would either use I=HILOTJ, or create an Annotate data set, which is assigned on the PROC GPLOT statement with ANNO=. However, I=HILOTJ and ANNO= are not permitted in Altair SLC, but, fortunately, ANNOTATE= can replace ANNO=.

```
PROC SORT DATA = sashelp9.class OUT = class_error;
   BY sex height;
RUN;

PROC SUMMARY DATA = class_error NWAY;
   CLASS sex;
   VAR weight;
   OUTPUT OUT = class_error_se STDERR = weight_se;
RUN;

DATA class_error_classic (KEEP = sex height value)
     class_error_ods
       (KEEP = sex height value value_upper value_lower);
   MERGE class_error class_error_se;
   BY sex;
   value = weight;
   value_upper = value + weight_se;
   value_lower = value - weight_se;
   OUTPUT class_error_ods;
   OUTPUT class_error_classic;
   value = value_upper;
   OUTPUT class_error_classic;
   value = value_lower;
   OUTPUT class_error_classic;
RUN;

%LET height_offset = 0.3;

DATA class_error_anno;
   SET class_error_ods;
   BY sex;
   LENGTH function $8
          color $20
          when xsys ysys $1
          x y 8
          ;
   xsys = '2';
   ysys = '2';
   when = 'A';
   IF sex = 'M' THEN color = 'RED';
   ELSE color = 'BLUE';
   function = 'MOVE';
   x = height - &height_offset.;
   y = value_upper;
   OUTPUT;
   function = 'DRAW';
   x = height + &height_offset.;
   y = value_upper;
   OUTPUT;
   function = 'MOVE';
   x = height;
   y = value_upper;
   OUTPUT;
```

```
        function = 'DRAW';
        x   height;
        y = value_lower;
        OUTPUT;
        function = 'MOVE';
        x = height - &height_offset.;
        y = value_lower;
        OUTPUT;
        function = 'DRAW';
        x = height + &height_offset.;
        y = value_lower;
        OUTPUT;
RUN;

PROC GPLOT DATA = class_error ANNOTATE = class_error_anno;
    SYMBOL V = CIRCLE I = JOIN;
    PLOT weight * height = sex / VAXIS = 40 TO 160 BY 10;
    LABEL weight = "Weight";
RUN;
```

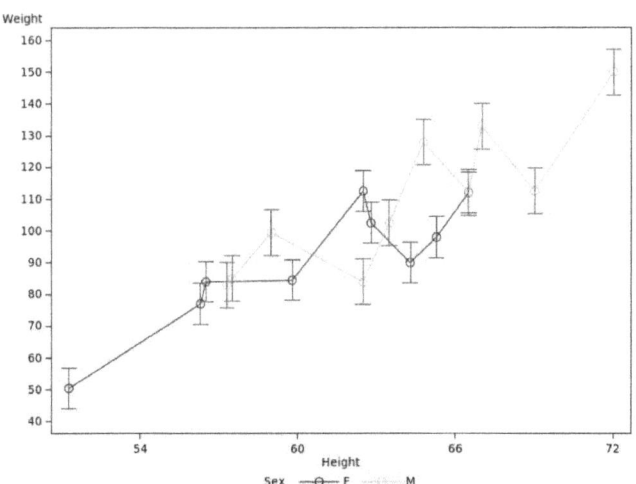

PROC SGPLOT

```
PROC SORT DATA = sashelp9.class OUT = class_error;
    BY sex height;
RUN;
```

```
PROC SUMMARY DATA = class_error NWAY;
    CLASS sex;
    VAR weight;
    OUTPUT OUT = class_error_se STDERR = weight_se;
RUN;
```

```
DATA class_error_ods
     (KEEP = sex height value value_upper value_lower);
     MERGE class_error class_error_se;
     BY sex;
     value = weight;
     value_upper = value + weight_se;
     value_lower = value - weight_se;
RUN;

PROC SGPLOT DATA = class_error_ods;
     SCATTER Y = value X = height
          / GROUP = sex YERRORUPPER = value_upper
               YERRORLOWER = value_lower;
     SERIES Y = value X = height / GROUP = sex;
     LABEL value = "Weight";
RUN;
```

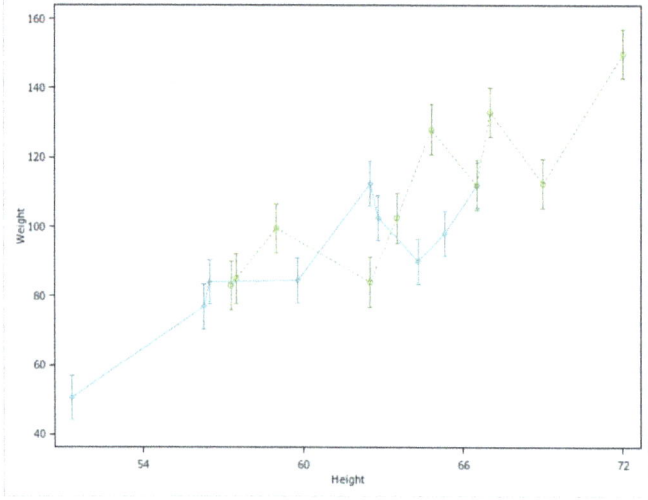

Box Plots

In SAS/GRAPH the box plots were thin and uninteresting, which meant you had to customise them. This is why most box plots are now created using ODS Graphics anyway.

The Altair SLC code only differs from the SAS/GRAPH code by using the SASHELP9 library reference, which refers to the SAS 9.4 installation libraries. By default, Altair SLC has a SASHELP library reference, which refers to its own system data sets.

PROC GPLOT

In the following program BOX00T has been commented out, because the SYMBOL statement in Altair SLC only includes the following values for I= (INTERPOL=): NONE, JOIN, NEEDLE, SPLINE, STEP or R. Therefore the "box plot" is not drawn, but a scatter plot is drawn instead using V=CIRCLE and I=NONE, which is unsatisfactory.

```
PROC SORT DATA = sashelp9.class
          OUT = class;
    BY age;
RUN;

PROC GPLOT DATA = class;
    SYMBOL V = CIRCLE I = NONE /*BOX00T*/;
    PLOT height * age;
RUN;
```

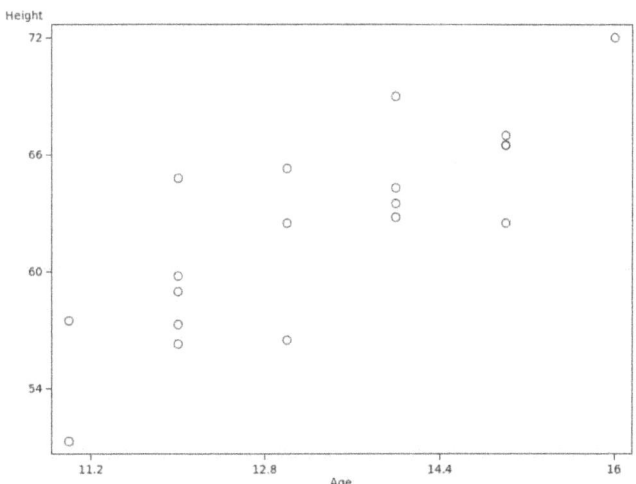

PROC SGPLOT

In Altair SLC, PROC SGPLOT generates a perfectly acceptable box plot with little effort:

```
PROC SORT DATA = sashelp9.class
          OUT = class;
    BY age;
RUN;
```

```
PROC SGPLOT DATA = class;
    VBOX height / CATEGORY = age;
RUN;
```

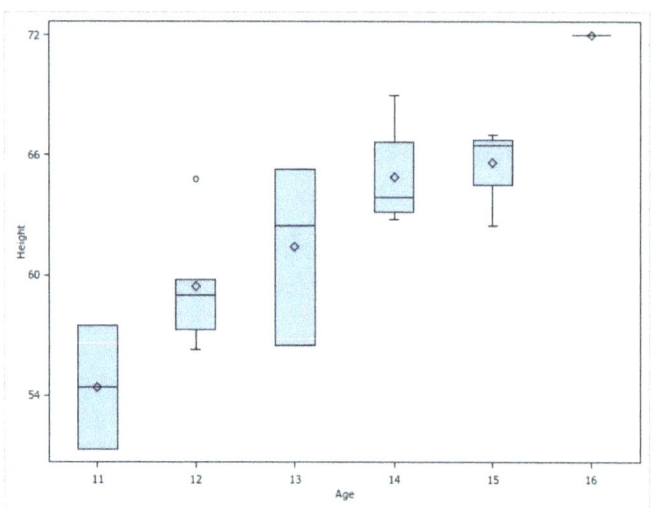

Vertical Bar Charts

The Altair SLC code only differs from the SAS/GRAPH code by using the SASHELP9 library reference, which refers to the SAS 9.4 installation libraries. By default, Altair SLC has a SASHELP library reference, which refers to its own system data sets.

Simple Vertical Bar Charts

PROC GCHART

```
PROC GCHART DATA = sashelp9.class;
    TITLE "PROC GCHART: Simple vertical barchart of CLASS";
    VBAR age / DISCRETE;
RUN;
```

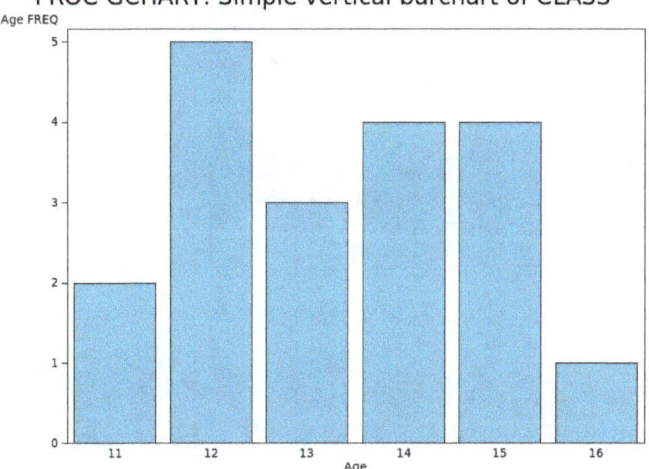

PROC SGPLOT

```
PROC SORT DATA = sashelp9.class
          OUT = class;
    BY sex age;
RUN;
```

```
PROC SGPLOT DATA = class;
   TITLE "PROC SGPLOT: Simple vertical barchart of CLASS";
   VBAR age;
RUN;
```

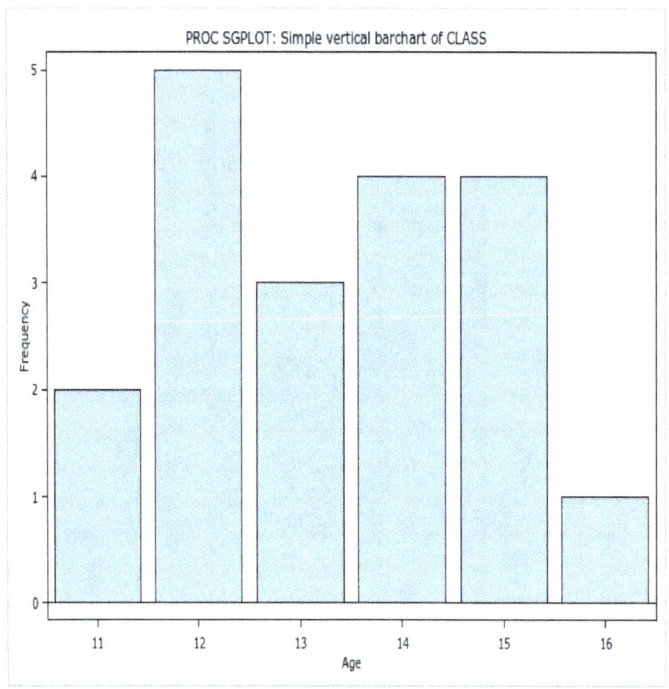

Stacked Vertical Bar Charts

PROC GCHART

```
PROC SORT DATA = sashelp9.class
          OUT = class;
   BY sex age;
RUN;
```

```
PROC GCHART DATA = class;
    TITLE "PROC GCHART: Stacked vertical barchart of CLASS";
    VBAR age / SUBGROUP = sex DISCRETE;
RUN;
```

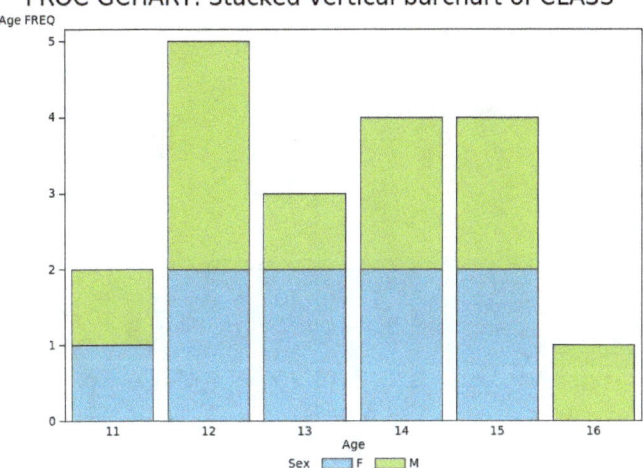

PROC SGPLOT

```
PROC SORT DATA = sashelp9.class
          OUT = class;
    BY sex age;
RUN;
```

70 Generating Graphics with Altair SLC

```
PROC SGPLOT DATA = class;
    TITLE "PROC SGPLOT: Stacked vertical barchart of CLASS";
    VBAR age / GROUP = sex;
RUN;
```

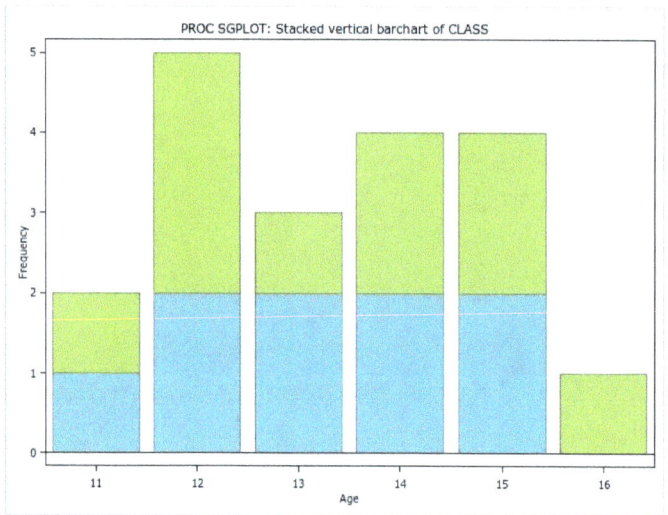

Clustered Vertical Bar Charts

PROC GCHART

```
PROC SORT DATA = sashelp9.class
          OUT = class;
    BY sex age;
RUN;

PROC GCHART DATA = class;
    TITLE "PROC GCHART: Clustered vertical barchart of
          CLASS";
    VBAR sex / GROUP = age
               PATTERNID = MIDPOINT;
RUN;
```

PROC GCHART: Clustered vertical barchart of CLASS

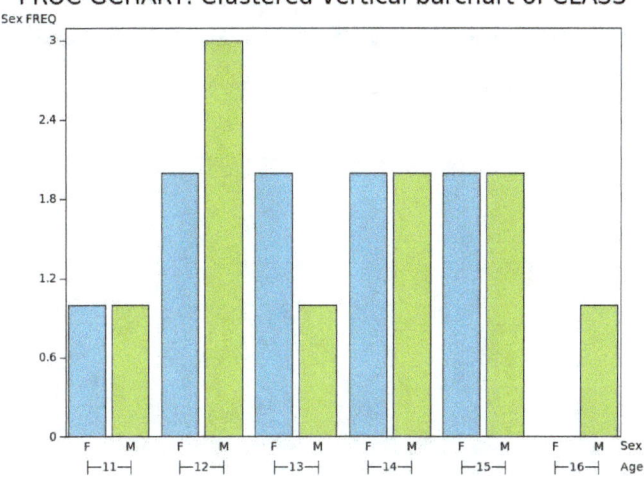

PROC SGPLOT

```
PROC SORT DATA = sashelp9.class
          OUT = class;
     BY sex age;
RUN;
```

72 Generating Graphics with Altair SLC

```
PROC SGPLOT DATA = class;
    TITLE
        "PROC SGPLOT: Clustered vertical barchart of CLASS";
    VBAR age / GROUP = sex
               GROUPDISPLAY = CLUSTER;
RUN;
```

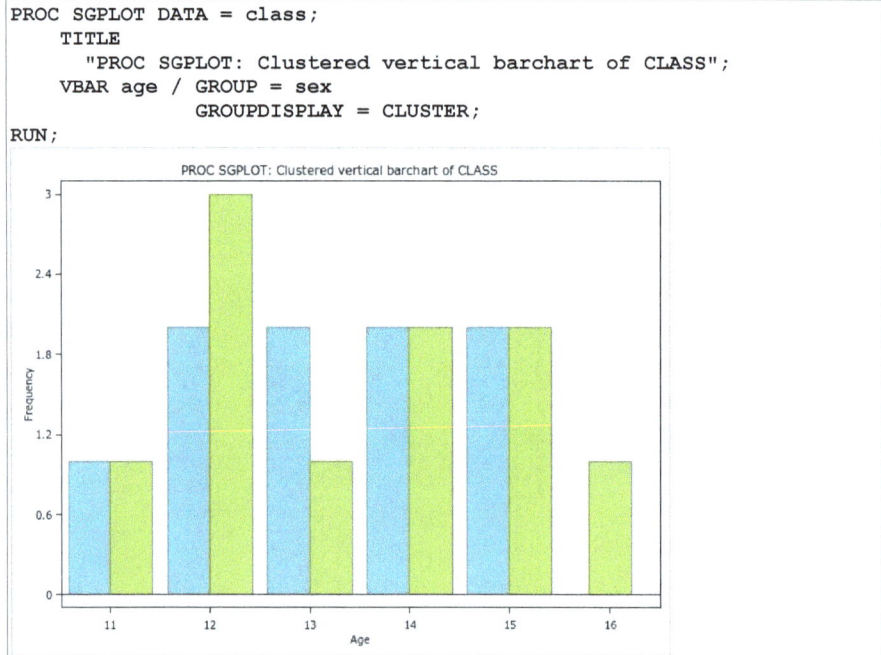

Horizontal Bar Charts

The Altair SLC code only differs from the SAS/GRAPH code by using the SASHELP9 library reference, which refers to the SAS 9.4 installation libraries. By default, Altair SLC has a SASHELP library reference, which refers to its own system data sets.

Simple Horizontal Bar Charts

PROC GCHART

```
PROC SORT DATA = sashelp9.class
          OUT = class;
    BY sex age;
RUN;

PROC GCHART DATA = class;
    TITLE
        "PROC GCHART: Simple horizontal barchart of CLASS";
    HBAR age / DISCRETE;
RUN;
```

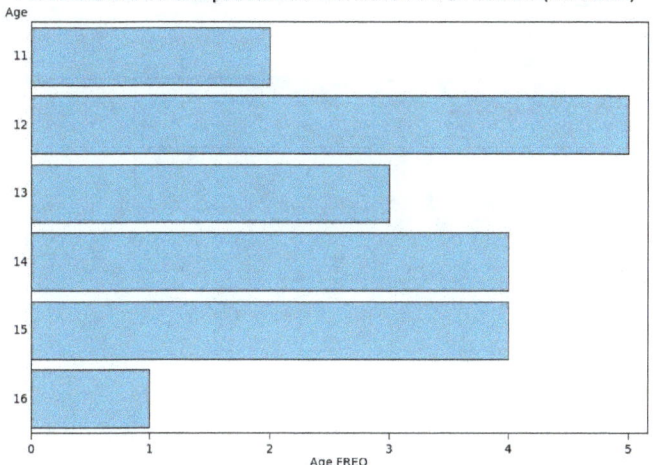

PROC GCHART: Simple horizontal barchart of CLASS (no stats)

PROC SGPLOT

```
PROC SORT DATA = sashelp9.class
          OUT = class;
    BY sex age;
RUN;

PROC SGPLOT DATA = class;
    TITLE
        "PROC SGPLOT: Simple horizontal barchart of CLASS";
    HBAR age;
RUN;
```

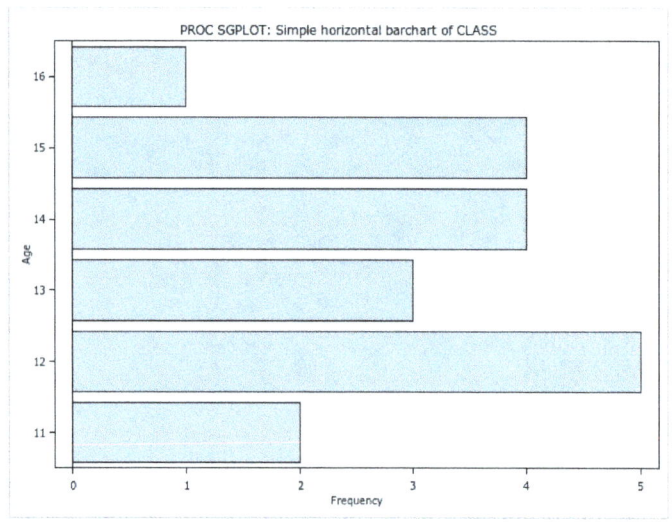

Stacked Horizontal Bar Charts

PROC GCHART

```
PROC SORT DATA = sashelp9.class
          OUT = class;
   BY sex age;
RUN;
```

```
PROC GCHART DATA = class;
    TITLE
       "PROC GCHART: Stacked horizontal barchart of CLASS";
    HBAR age / SUBGROUP = sex DISCRETE;
RUN;
```

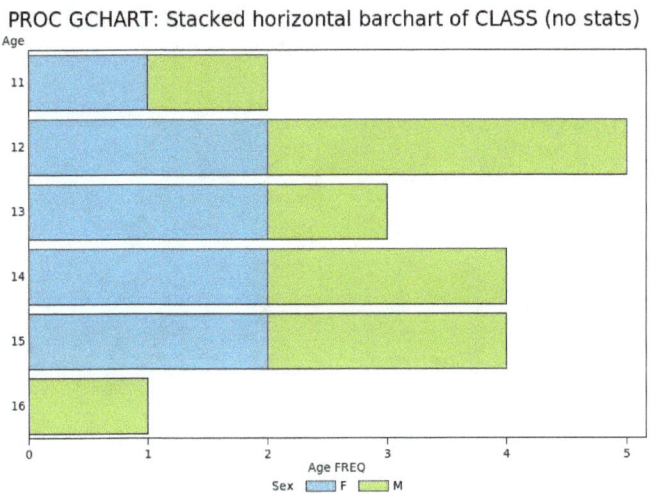

PROC SGPLOT

By default Altair SLC assumes that the KEYLEGEND is not required for PROC SGPLOT, which is the opposite of SAS software, so /*WPS*/ is used to mark the extra statement.

```
PROC SORT DATA = sashelp9.class
          OUT = class;
    BY sex age;
RUN;
```

76 Generating Graphics with Altair SLC

```
PROC SGPLOT DATA = class;
   TITLE
      "PROC SGPLOT: Stacked horizontal barchart of CLASS";
   HBAR age / GROUP = sex;
   KEYLEGEND;  /*WPS*/
RUN;
```

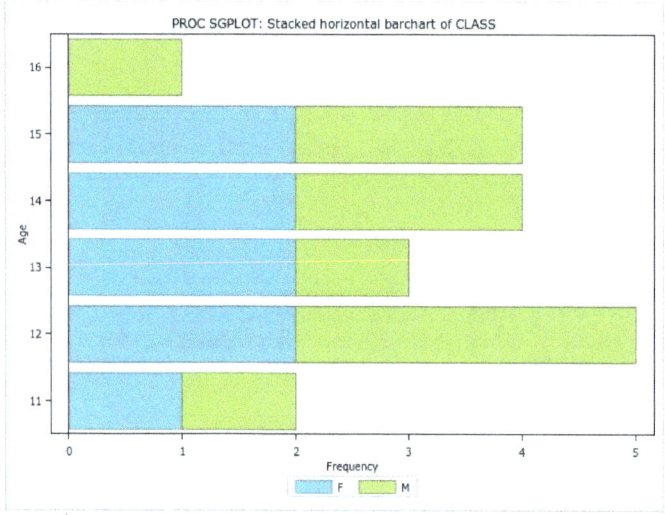

Clustered Horizontal Bar Charts

PROC GCHART

```
PROC SORT DATA = sashelp9.class
          OUT = class;
   BY sex age;
RUN;
```

```
PROC GCHART DATA = class;
   TITLE
      "PROC GCHART: Clustered horizontal barchart of CLASS";
   HBAR sex / GROUP = age
              PATTERNID = MIDPOINT;
RUN;
```

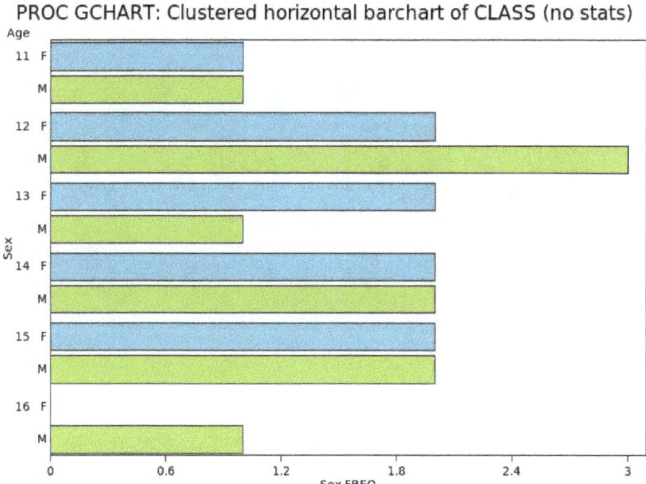

PROC SGPLOT

By default Altair SLC assumes that the KEYLEGEND is not required for PROC SGPLOT, which is the opposite of SAS software, so /*WPS*/ is used to mark the extra statement.

```
PROC SORT DATA = sashelp9.class
          OUT = class;
   BY sex age;
RUN;

PROC SGPLOT DATA = class;
   TITLE
      "PROC SGPLOT: Clustered horizontal barchart of CLASS";
   HBAR age / GROUP = sex
              GROUPDISPLAY = CLUSTER;
   KEYLEGEND;   /*WPS*/
RUN;
```

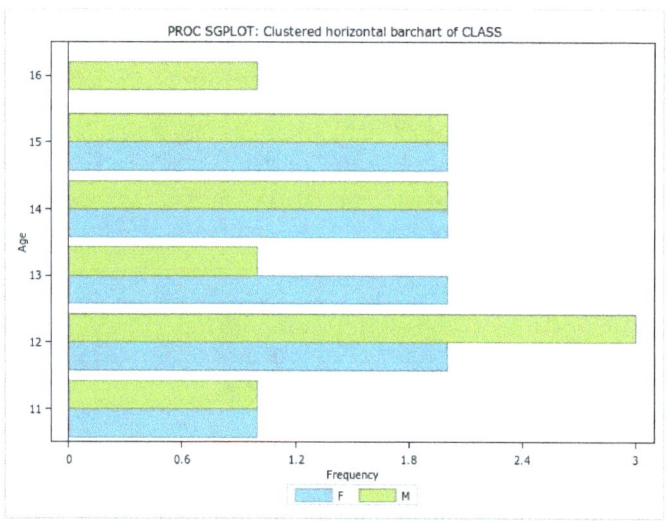

2D Pie Charts

There are actually 3 ways of generating 2D Pie Charts in Altair SLC, as there are in the latest SAS software:

- PROC GCHART

- PROC TEMPLATE and PROC SGRENDER

- PROC SGPIE

The choice is up to you, as they are all perfectly acceptable.

The Altair SLC code only differs from the SAS/GRAPH code by using the SASHELP9 library reference, which refers to the SAS 9.4 installation libraries. By default, Altair SLC has its own SASHELP library reference, which refers to its own system data sets.

PROC GCHART

In the following program LEGEND has been commented out, because the PIE statement in Altair SLC does not include it.

```
PROC SORT DATA = sashelp9.class
          OUT = class;
    BY age;
RUN;

PROC GCHART DATA = class;
    PIE age / VALUE = ARROW
              /*LEGEND*/ DISCRETE;
RUN;
```

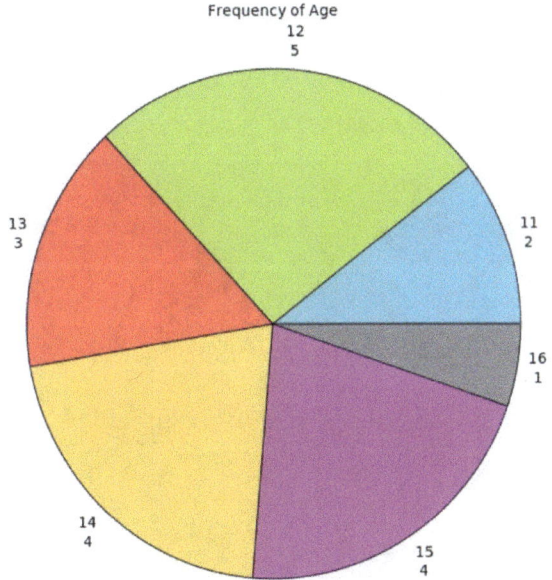

PROC TEMPLATE and PROC SGRENDER

There is a similarity with the image generated by PROC GCHART, albeit mirrored, because I have explicitly used START=180 and CATEGORYDIRECTION=CLOCKWISE, whereas the default in PROC GCHART is anti-clockwise starting at angle=0.

```
PROC SORT DATA = sashelp9.class
          OUT = class;
    BY age;
RUN;
```

80 Generating Graphics with Altair SLC

```
PROC TEMPLATE;
  DEFINE STATGRAPH pie;
    BEGINGRAPH;
      LAYOUT REGION;
        PIECHART CATEGORY = age /
          DATALABELLOCATION = OUTSIDE
          CATEGORYDIRECTION = CLOCKWISE
          START = 180 NAME = 'pie';
        DISCRETELEGEND 'pie' /
          TITLE = 'Age';
      ENDLAYOUT;
    ENDGRAPH;
  END;
RUN;

PROC SGRENDER DATA = class TEMPLATE = pie;
RUN;
```

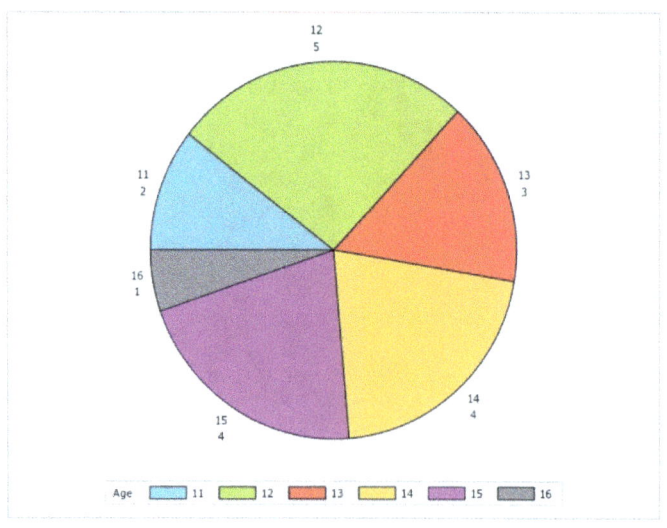

PROC SGPIE

I have not mentioned PROC SGPIE in any previous papers or books, but the new procedure has been included in Altair SLC. You will immediately see the similarity with the image generated by PROC TEMPLATE and PROC SGRENDER, albeit mirrored, because of CATEGORYDIRECTION=COUNTERCLOCKWISE and START=0 (which is the default in PROC GCHART). Please note that the KEYLEGEND statement is needed to generate the legend (marked with /*WPS*/), unlike in SAS, where showing the legend is the default setting.

By default Altair SLC assumes that the KEYLEGEND is not required for PROC SGPLOT, which is the opposite of SAS software, so /*WPS*/ is used to mark the extra statement.

```
PROC SORT DATA = sashelp9.class
          OUT = class;
     BY age;
RUN;

PROC SGPIE DATA = class;
     TITLE "PROC SGPIE: Pie chart of CLASS";
     PIE age / STAT = FREQ STARTANGLE = 0
               DATALABELLOCATION = OUTSIDE
               CATEGORYDIRECTION = COUNTERCLOCKWISE;
     KEYLEGEND;   /*WPS*/
RUN;
```

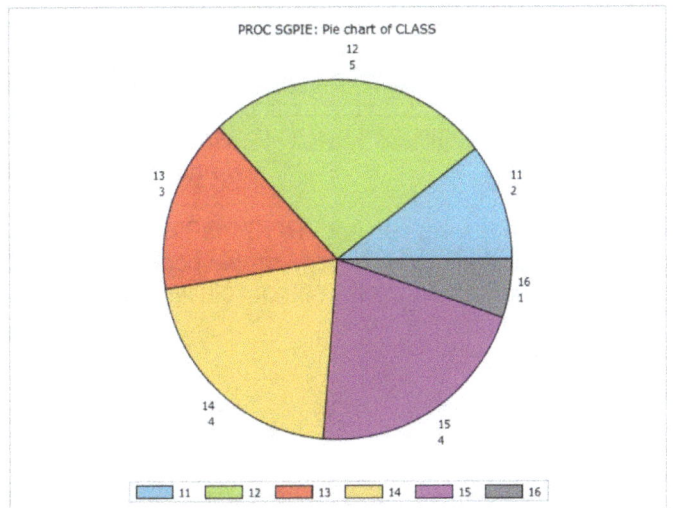

It should also be noted that, due to the different options available in PROC SGPIE in SAS software and Altair SLC, the Altair SLC program above will not work in SAS software:

- DATALABELLOCATION= is DATALABELLOC= in SAS software.
- CATEGORYDIRECTION= is DIRECTION= in SAS software.
- STAT=FREQ is not needed in SAS software.

Conclusions

- Apart from changing **sashelp** to **sashelp9**, which references the SAS software versions of the SASHELP library, the same code as works in SAS 9.4 also works in Altair SLC, unless otherwise stated.

- Most of the PROC SGPLOT graphs are replicated with minimal changes, although the legends may need to be explicitly requested in Altair SLC.

- Some SYMBOL options are not included in Altair SLC, so regression, error bar, and box plots must be created using PROC SGPLOT, rather than using PROC GPLOT.

- In SAS 9.4 the tick marks on the axes in SAS/GRAPH were significantly different from those generated in ODS Graphics. However, the tick marks on the axes in Altair SLC are found to be the same in PROC GPLOT, PROC GCHART, PROC SGPLOT, PROC SGPANEL, PROC SGSCATTER and PROC SGRENDER.

- Altair SLC includes the newest PROC SGPIE, which generates an acceptable 2D Pie Chart with very simple code. However, this procedure is not currently very compatible with SAS software.

Using Altair SLC with R and Python

Introduction

Altair SLC uses a single software licence that includes interfaces to R and Python. In SAS software an additional SAS/IML licence would be required, as connections to R and Python are not included in Base SAS. This means that, by default, all SAS programs run in Altair SLC can incorporate R and/or Python functionality.

In 2005 I had attended a seminar about combining S-plus and SAS to create "trellis" graphs. This was before the introduction of ODS Graphics in SAS 9.1.3, so SAS could only create "trellis" graphs in SAS/GRAPH by using PROC GREPLAY, which lacked the flexibility to plot an unknown number of individual plots programmatically. I was reluctant to license S-plus, but, as R software was free and was a closely related language, I chose R to look at how "trellis" plots could be sent to an ODS destination.

SAS Software and R

Back in 2005, after SAS Forum International had stopped organising technical conferences in Europe, my paper "SAS to R to SAS" was presented as a paper and a poster at the inaugural PhUSE (Pharmaceutical Users Software Exchange) in Heidelberg, Germany. It was to be the first of 13 consecutive PhUSE conferences where I was a presenter.

Software Environment

- The examples described in the original paper used Windows XP, but any platform compatible with SAS and R could have been used.

- The methods can be used in any version of Base SAS from version 7 onwards. No other licensed SAS components are required.

- R requires 2 non-standard add-on libraries to be installed to support the techniques used in this paper. The "**Hmisc**" library adds R functions to import "foreign" data into R, e.g. SAS data, comma-separated value (CSV) data, etc. The library requires an additional SAS macro, **%exportlib**, which can be used to export a folder of SAS data sets into a collection of CSV files to be read into R using the **sasxport.get** function. The "**lattice**" library adds R functions to create "trellis" graphics. The "**grDevices**" library is supplied as part of the R system and includes functions to create a variety of image file formats, including JPEG, GIF and PNG.

Program Flow

Select the SAS data set to transfer and save the data set to a folder:

```
LIBNAME new 'c:\temp\new';

PROC DATASETS LIB = new KILL;
RUN;
QUIT;

DATA sasuser.v_prdsale / VIEW = sasuser.v_prdsale;
  SET sashelp.prdsale;
  LENGTH yyq $6;
  yyqtr = year + (quarter - 1)/4;
  mon = MONTH(month);
  yyq = PUT(month, YYQ6.);
  yq = INTCK('QTR', '31dec1992'd, month);
  SELECT (country);
    WHEN ('U.S.A.') cntry = 'USA';
    WHEN ('GERMANY') cntry = 'DE';
    WHEN ('CANADA') cntry = 'CA';
    OTHERWISE;
  END;
RUN;

PROC SUMMARY DATA = sasuser.v_prdsale MISSING NWAY;
  CLASS cntry yq product;
  VAR actual;
  OUTPUT OUT = new.prdsale SUM =;
RUN;
```

Export the folder to CSV files (using **%exportlib**), including the contents of the folder and data for any SAS user-defined formats. Note that the folders must be written with '/' separators, even if you are running the program in Windows. The macro exports all SAS data sets in a data library to CSV files. One of the data sets is assumed to be the result of PROC FORMAT CNTLOUT= if any user formats are referenced. Numeric variables are formatted in BEST16. format so that date/time variables will be exported with their internal numeric values. A special file _contents_.csv is created to hold, for all data sets combined, the data set name, data set label, variable names, labels, formats, types, and lengths.

```
/* Macro exportlib
   Usage: %exportlib(lib, outdir, tempdir);
   Arguments:
     lib - SAS libname for input data sets
     outdir - directory in which to write .csv files
       (default ".")
     tempdir - temporary directory to hold generated
       SAS code (default C:/WINDOWS/TEMP)
*/
%MACRO exportlib(lib, outdir, tempdir);
  %IF %QUOTE(&outdir)= %THEN %LET outdir=.;
  %IF %QUOTE(&tempdir)=
    %THEN %LET tempdir=C:/WINDOWS/TEMP;
  OPTIONS NOFMTERR;

  PROC COPY IN = &lib OUT = work;
  RUN;

  PROC CONTENTS DATA = work._ALL_ NOPRINT
    OUT = _contents_(KEEP = memname memlabel name type
                            label format length nobs);
  RUN;

  PROC EXPORT DATA = _contents_
    OUTFILE = "&outdir/_contents_.csv" REPLACE;
  RUN;

  DATA _NULL_;
    SET _contents_;
    BY memname;
    FILE "&tempdir/_export_.sas";
    RETAIN bk -1;
    IF FIRST.memname & (nobs > 0) THEN DO;
      PUT 'DATA ' memname ';';
      PUT ' SET ' memname ';';
      PUT ' FORMAT _NUMERIC_ BEST14.;';
      PUT 'RUN;';
```

```
        PUT 'PROC EXPORT DATA = ' memname;
        PUT ' OUTFILE = "' "&outdir/" memname
            +bk '.csv"';
        PUT ' REPLACE;';
        PUT 'RUN;';
      END;
   RUN;

   %INCLUDE "&tempdir/_export_.sas";
   %MEND exportlib;

   PROC FORMAT CNTLOUT = _cntlout;
   RUN;

   %exportlib(new, c:/temp/r, c:/windows/temp);
```

Generate R code (including **sasxport.get**) to read CSV files and write the generated graph to a JPEG file of 480x480 pixels:

```
DATA _NULL_;
  FILE 'c:\temp\r\program.r' LRECL = 1024;
  PUT 'library(Hmisc)';
  PUT 'library(lattice)';
  PUT 'library(grDevices)';
  PUT "sasdata <- sasxport.get('c:/temp/r',";
  PUT "   method=('csv'))";
  PUT "trellis.device(jpeg,
         file='c:/temp/r/program.jpg',";
  PUT '   width=480, height=480)';
  PUT 'trellis.par.set(theme=col.whitebg())';
  PUT "trellis.par.set('background',
         list(col='white'))";
  PUT "trellis.par.set('plot.symbol',
         list(col='blue'))";
  PUT "trellis.par.set('dot.symbol',
         list(col='blue'))";
  PUT "trellis.par.set('axis.line', list(col='red'))";
  PUT "trellis.par.set('box.rectangle',
                  list(col='red'))";
  PUT "trellis.par.set('par.xlab.text',
                  list(col='green'))";
  PUT "trellis.par.set('par.ylab.text',
                  list(col='green'))";
  PUT "trellis.par.set('par.zlab.text',
                  list(col='green'))";
  PUT "trellis.par.set('axis.text',
                  list(col='green'))";
  PUT 'xyplot(actual ~ yq | product*cntry,';
  PUT '   data=sasdata$prdsale,';
  PUT "   xlab = 'Quarter',";
  PUT "   ylab = 'Actual Sales',";
  PUT '   panel = function(x, y) {';
  PUT '     panel.grid(h=-1, v=-1)';
  PUT '     panel.xyplot(x, y)';
```

Altair SLC 87

```
PUT '      panel.loess(x, y,';
PUT '         span=1,';
PUT '         degree=2';
PUT '      )';
PUT '   },';
PUT "   main = 'Plotted using R'";
PUT ')';
PUT 'dev.off()';
PUT 'q()';
RUN;
```

Execute R command line, including R code file as the input program. In this case the R program can be found in the Windows default program path:

```
OPTIONS XWAIT XSYNC;
X "r.exe --no-save --quiet <""c:\temp\r\program.r""
  >""c:\temp\r\program.log""";
```

Execute R code, outputting R log to a text file and the graph to a JPEG file. Note that the white background is required for most ODS Styles to allow the resulting graphs to appear consistent with each other. The default background for R graphs is a light grey:

```
library(Hmisc)
library(lattice)
library(grDevices)
sasdata <- sasxport.get('c:/temp/r',
                       method=('csv'))
trellis.device(jpeg, file='c:/temp/r/program.jpg',
               width=480, height=480)
trellis.par.set(theme=col.whitebg())
trellis.par.set('background', list(col='white'))
trellis.par.set('plot.symbol', list(col='blue'))
trellis.par.set('dot.symbol', list(col='blue'))
trellis.par.set('axis.line', list(col='red'))
trellis.par.set('box.rectangle', list(col='red'))
trellis.par.set('par.xlab.text', list(col='green'))
trellis.par.set('par.ylab.text', list(col='green'))
trellis.par.set('axis.text', list(col='green'))
```

```
xyplot(actual ~ yq | product*cntry,
       data=sasdata$prdsale,
  xlab = 'Quarter',
  ylab = 'Actual Sales',
  panel = function(x, y) {
    panel.grid(h=-1, v=-1)
    panel.xyplot(x, y)
    panel.loess(x, y,
                span=1,
                degree=2
  },
  main = 'Plotted using R'
)
dev.off()
```

Close R session:

```
q()
```

Copy the R log file into the SAS log:

```
DATA _NULL_;
  INFILE 'c:\temp\r\program.log';
  FILE LOG;
  INPUT;
  PUT '**R: ' _INFILE_;
RUN;
```

Open the ODS destination, e.g. HTML:

```
ODS ESCAPECHAR = '^';
ODS HTML FILE = 'c:\temp\r\report.html'
         STYLE = minimal GPATH = 'c:\temp\r'
         NOGTITLE NOGFOOTNOTE;
```

or RTF:

```
ODS ESCAPECHAR = '^';
ODS RTF FILE = 'c:\temp\r\report.rtf' STYLE = minimal
         NOGTITLE NOGFOOTNOTE;
```

Incorporate the JPEG file in the SAS report in HTML:

```
DATA _NULL_;
  FILE PRINT;
  PUT "<IMG SRC='c:\temp\r\program.jpg' BORDER='0'>";
RUN;
```

or RTF:

```
DATA _NULL_;
  FILE PRINT;
  PUT "^S={PREIMAGE='c:\temp\r\program.jpg'}";
RUN;
```

Close the ODS destination:

```
ODS _ALL_ CLOSE;
```

This generates the following image in the ODS destination:

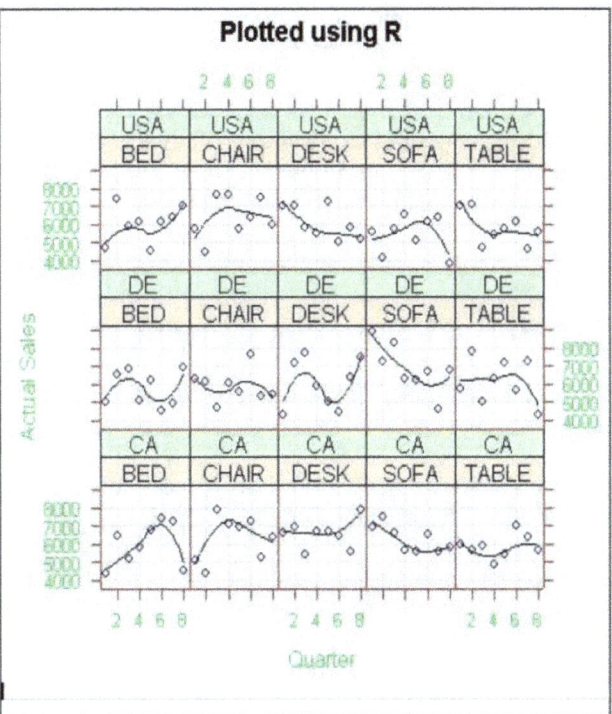

Coding Issues

As an experienced SAS programmer, but an inexperienced R programmer, I had to resolve the following issues while developing this reporting application:

- HTML reports require a different syntax for displaying external image files to that used for non-HTML reports, e.g. RTF, PDF, etc., so the code must include separate code sections for use with HTML and non-HTML destinations.

- As different output destinations have different acceptable image formats, try to select a compatible image format for all of the expected output destinations.

- As the export processing creates CSV files for every SAS data set in the specified folder, limiting the number of SAS data sets in that folder will reduce the run time required for the R code to import the data.

- The R code is executed by calling the R system in line-command mode using the SAS X statement. The XSYNC and XWAIT SAS System options must be set before calling R.

- R programs may fail with minimal error information in the R log file.

Altair SLC and R Software Environment

- The example described below uses Windows 11, but any platform compatible with Altair SLC and R could have been used.

- The methods can be used in any version of Altair SLC (WPS) from version 4 onwards, which includes PROC R.

- R requires just one non-standard add-on library: the **lattice** library, which adds R functions to create "trellis" graphics.

Differences between SAS Software and Altair SLC

- Whereas the original SAS program included converting SAS data sets to CSV to input into the R program, PROC R in Altair SLC allows the transfer of SAS data sets directly into R.

- The original SAS program required another library in R to convert the "trellis" image to JPEG to pass back into SAS. Images in PROC R in Altair SLC can be passed directly into the output.

- Altair SLC does not include the **sashelp** data sets, so **sashelp.prdsale** from SAS software has been copied to **sashelp9.prdsale**.

Program Flow

Specify where the R software is installed using OPTIONS SET=:

Altair SLC **91**

```
OPTIONS SET = R_HOME 'F:\Program Files\R\R-4.3.0';
```

Select the SAS data set to use in R:

```
DATA sasuser.v_prdsale / VIEW = sasuser.v_prdsale;
   SET sashelp9.prdsale;
   LENGTH yyq $6;
   yyqtr = year + (quarter - 1) / 4;
   mon = MONTH(month);
   yyq = PUT(month, YYQ6.);
   yq = INTCK('QTR', '31dec1992'd, month);
   SELECT (country);
      WHEN ('U.S.A.') cntry = 'USA';
      WHEN ('GERMANY') cntry = 'DE';
      WHEN ('CANADA') cntry = 'CA';
      OTHERWISE;
   END;
RUN;

PROC SUMMARY DATA = sasuser.v_prdsale MISSING NWAY;
   CLASS cntry yq product;
   VAR actual;
   OUTPUT OUT = prdsale SUM =;
RUN;

PROC PRINT DATA = prdsale;
   TITLE 'PRDSALE summary';
RUN;
```

Set up the output folders using ODS HTML, where NOGTITLE and NOGFOOTNOTE have been used, because PROC R does not honour these options:

```
ODS ESCAPECHAR = '^';

ODS HTML FILE = "./r_xyplot_WPS.html"
         STYLE = minimal GPATH = "./images"
         NOGTITLE NOGFOOTNOTE;
```

Execute R code, outputting the R log directly back to the SAS Log and the output to the open ODS destination. Note that the white background is required for most ODS Styles to allow the resulting graphs to appear consistent with each other. The default background for R graphs is a light grey: Unlike in SAS, continuing statements in PROC R must end in ",".

```
PROC R TERMINATE;
   EXPORT DATA = prdsale R = sasdata;
   SUBMIT;
      library(lattice)
      print(sasdata)
```

Using Altair SLC with R and Python

```
   trellis.par.set(theme = col.whitebg())
   trellis.par.set('background', list(col = 'white'))
   trellis.par.set('plot.symbol', list(col = 'blue'))
   trellis.par.set('dot.symbol', list(col = 'blue'))
   trellis.par.set('axis.line', list(col = 'red'))
   trellis.par.set('box.rectangle',
                   list(col = 'red'))
   trellis.par.set('par.xlab.text',
                   list(col = 'green'))
   trellis.par.set('par.ylab.text',
                   list(col = 'green'))
   trellis.par.set('par.zlab.text',
                   list(col = 'green'))
   trellis.par.set('axis.text', list(col = 'green'))
   xyplot(ACTUAL ~ yq | PRODUCT * cntry,
     data = sasdata,
     xlab = 'Quarter',
     ylab = 'Actual Sales',
     panel = function(x, y) {
       panel.grid(h = -1, v = -1)
       panel.xyplot(x, y)
       panel.loess(x, y, span = 1, degree = 2)
     },
     main = 'Plotted using R'
   )
  ENDSUBMIT;
RUN;
```

Close the ODS destination:

```
ODS HTML CLOSE;
```

The following image is created by Altair SLC:

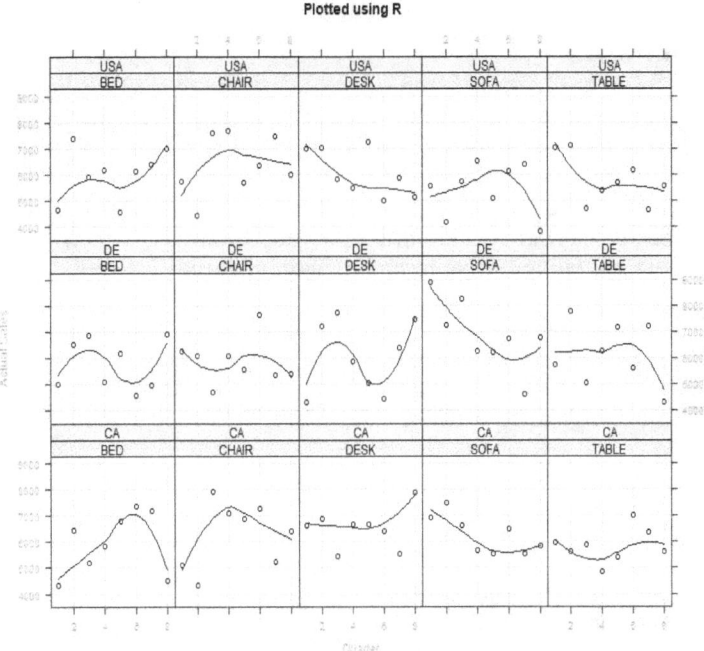

Altair SLC and Python Software Environment

- The example described below uses Windows 11, but any platform compatible with Altair SLC and Python could have been used.

- The methods can be used in any version of Altair SLC (WPS) from version 4 onwards, which includes PROC PYTHON.

- PROC PYTHON requires just 2 add-on libraries: the "**pandas**" and "**numpy**" libraries, which add Python functions to translate SAS data sets into Python dataframes.

- The following program also requires the "**matplotlib**" and "**seaborn**" libraries for the graphics.

- The "**pandas**", "**numpy**" and "**matplotlib**" libraries can be installed with Python software when installing the Anaconda suite.

- The "**seaborn**" library should be installed using the `pip install seaborn` command in Anaconda.

Program Flow

You will recognise some of the data processing steps prior to PROC PYTHON, as these were also used with PROC R above.

Specify where the Python software is installed using OPTIONS PYTHONHOME=: This is different from accessing R, which required an environment variable to be set to the location of R.

```
OPTIONS PYTHONHOME = 'F:\ProgramData\anaconda3';
```

Select the SAS data set to use in Python:

```
DATA sasuser.v_prdsale / VIEW = sasuser.v_prdsale;
  SET sashelp9.prdsale;
  LENGTH yyq $6;
  yyqtr = year + (quarter - 1) / 4;
  mon = MONTH(month);
  yyq = PUT(month, YYQ6.);
  yq = INTCK('QTR', '31dec1992'd, month);
  SELECT (country);
    WHEN ('U.S.A.') cntry = 'USA';
    WHEN ('GERMANY') cntry = 'DE';
    WHEN ('CANADA') cntry = 'CA';
    OTHERWISE;
  END;
RUN;

PROC SUMMARY DATA = sasuser.v_prdsale MISSING NWAY;
  CLASS cntry yq product;
  VAR actual;
  OUTPUT OUT = prdsale SUM =;
RUN;

PROC PRINT DATA = prdsale;
  TITLE 'PRDSALE summary';
RUN;
```

Set up the output folders using ODS HTML, where NOGTITLE and NOGFOOTNOTE have been used, because PROC PYTHON does not honour these options:

```
TITLE 'Title specified in SAS program';

ODS ESCAPECHAR = '^';

ODS HTML FILE = "./python_seaborn_WPS.html"
         STYLE = minimal GPATH = "./images"
         NOGTITLE NOGFOOTNOTE;
```

or ODS PDF:

```
ODS PDF FILE = "./python_seaborn_WPS.pdf"
          STYLE = minimal NOGTITLE NOGFOOTNOTE;
```

Execute Python code, outputting the Python log directly back to the SAS Log and the output to the open ODS destination.

Note that R uses the LOESS (locally estimated scatterplot smoothing) smoothing method, whereas Python uses the LOWESS (locally weighted scatterplot smoothing) smoothing method. LOESS has not yet been implemented in a Python library. Also note that, while PROC R automatically outputs everything to ODS destinations, PROC PYTHON will automatically output text-based results to ODS destinations, but images must be sent to a special location called **wpsgloc** from within Python.

Please be aware that Python requires statements to start in column 1 (unlike SAS and R), and continuing statements in PROC PYTHON must end in ",".

```
PROC PYTHON TERMINATE;
   EXPORT DATA = prdsale PYTHON = sasdata;
   SUBMIT;

import seaborn as sns
import matplotlib.pyplot as plt
from matplotlib.gridspec import GridSpec
from statsmodels.nonparametric.smoothers_lowess import lowess
import os
print(sasdata)

# Set the overall aesthetic parameters
sns.set_palette(['blue'])
sns.set_style('white', {'axes.edgecolor': 'red',
     'axes.linewidth': 1, 'xtick.color': 'green',
     'ytick.color': 'green'})
plt.rcParams.update({'axes.labelcolor': 'green',
     'axes.titlesize': 12, 'axes.titleweight': 'bold'})

# Create the FacetGrid
g = sns.FacetGrid(sasdata, col="PRODUCT", row="cntry",
                  despine=False)
g.map(plt.scatter, 'yq', 'ACTUAL', color='blue')
```

```
# Adding LOWESS smoother manually for each subplot
for ax in g.axes.flat:
    # Extract title and relevant data
    row_val = ax.get_title().split(' | ')[0].split(' = ')[1]
    col_val = ax.get_title().split(' | ')[1].split(' = ')[1]
    ax.set_title(row_val.strip() + '\n' + col_val.strip())
    data = sasdata[(sasdata['PRODUCT'] == col_val) &
                   (sasdata['cntry'] == row_val)]
    # Sort data by x axis (yq)
    data_sorted = data.sort_values('yq')
    lowess_result = lowess(data_sorted['ACTUAL'],
                           data_sorted['yq'], frac=1)

    # Plot LOWESS line
    ax.plot(data_sorted['yq'], lowess_result[:, 1],
            color='red')
# Set axis labels and main title
g.set_axis_labels("Quarter", "Actual Sales")
g.fig.suptitle('Plotted using Python', fontsize=16)

# Adjust layout to make room for the main title
# and cell headers
plt.subplots_adjust(top=0.8, hspace=0.3)

# Save plot
plt.savefig(os.path.join(wpsgloc, 'python_seaborn_WPS.png'))

    ENDSUBMIT;
RUN;
```

Close the ODS HTML destination:

```
ODS HTML CLOSE;
```

or ODS PDF:

```
ODS PDF CLOSE;
```

The following page is created in the PDF file:

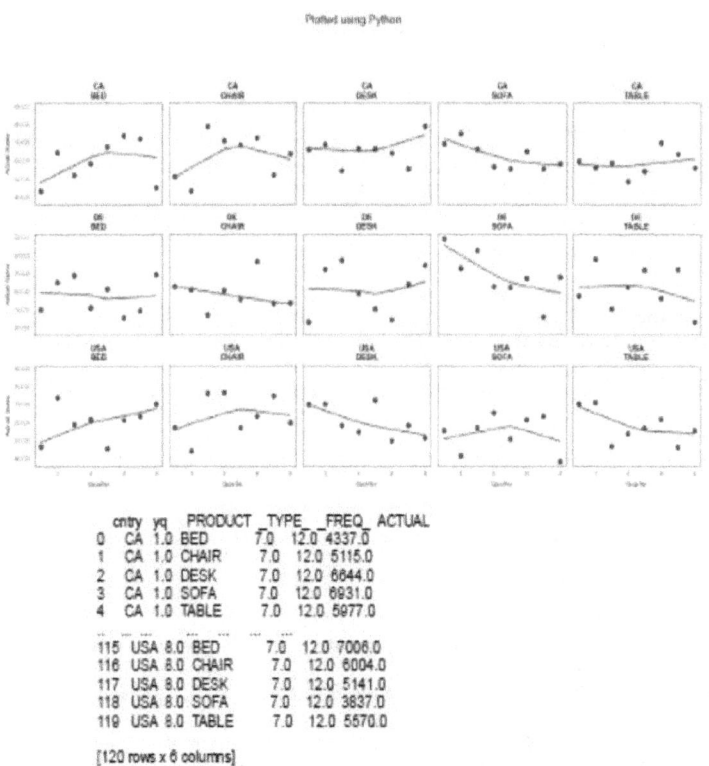

Note also that the `print(sasdata)` statement has generated a table after the trellis graph, even though the Python code was executed the other way around!

To fix this problem we can use a feature of PROC PYTHON, when run after OPTIONS PYTHONKEEP, which keeps the session active in the background between PROC PYTHON calls. Adding ODS PDF STARTPAGE=NOW before the second call will force the table to be sent to the ODS destination first.

```
TITLE 'Title specified in SAS program';

ODS ESCAPECHAR = '^';

OPTIONS PYTHONKEEP;

ODS PDF FILE = "./python_seaborn_WPS2.pdf"
        STYLE = minimal NOGTITLE NOGFOOTNOTE;

PROC PYTHON;
  EXPORT DATA = prdsale PYTHON = sasdata;
  SUBMIT;

import seaborn as sns
import matplotlib.pyplot as plt
from matplotlib.gridspec import GridSpec
from statsmodels.nonparametric.smoothers_lowess import lowess
import os
print(sasdata)

  ENDSUBMIT;
RUN;

ODS PDF STARTPAGE = NOW;

PROC PYTHON TERMINATE;
  SUBMIT;

# Set the overall aesthetic parameters
sns.set_palette(['blue'])
sns.set_style('white', {'axes.edgecolor': 'red',
    'axes.linewidth': 1, 'xtick.color': 'green',
    'ytick.color': 'green'})
plt.rcParams.update({'axes.labelcolor': 'green',
    'axes.titlesize': 12, 'axes.titleweight': 'bold'})

# Create the FacetGrid
g = sns.FacetGrid(sasdata, col="PRODUCT", row="cntry",
                  despine=False)
g.map(plt.scatter, 'yq', 'ACTUAL', color='blue')
```

Altair SLC **99**

```
# Adding LOWESS smoother manually for each subplot
for ax in g.axes.flat:
    # Extract title and relevant data
    row_val = ax.get_title().split(' | ')[0].split(' = ')[1]
    col_val = ax.get_title().split(' | ')[1].split(' = ')[1]
    ax.set_title(row_val.strip() + '\n' + col_val.strip())
    data = sasdata[(sasdata['PRODUCT'] == col_val) &
                   (sasdata['cntry'] == row_val)]
    # Sort data by x axis (yq)
    data_sorted = data.sort_values('yq')
    lowess_result = lowess(data_sorted['ACTUAL'],
                           data_sorted['yq'], frac=1)

    # Plot LOWESS line
    ax.plot(data_sorted['yq'], lowess_result[:, 1],
            color='red')

# Set axis labels and main title
g.set_axis_labels("Quarter", "Actual Sales")
g.fig.suptitle('Plotted using Python', fontsize=16)

# Adjust layout to make room for the main title
# and cell headers
plt.subplots_adjust(top=0.8, hspace=0.3)

# Save plot
plt.savefig(os.path.join(wpsgloc,
            'python_seaborn_WPS2.png'))

    ENDSUBMIT;
RUN;

ODS PDF CLOSE;
```

The following 2 pages are now created by Altair SLC, and in the correct order:

Title specified in SAS program   14:02 Saturday, June 1, 2024 1

```
     cntry yq  PRODUCT _TYPE_ _FREQ_  ACTUAL
  0  CA   1.0  BED       7.0   12.0   4337.0
  1  CA   1.0  CHAIR     7.0   12.0   5115.0
  2  CA   1.0  DESK      7.0   12.0   6644.0
  3  CA   1.0  SOFA      7.0   12.0   6931.0
  4  CA   1.0  TABLE     7.0   12.0   5977.0
 ..  ..   ..   ...       ...   ...    ...
115  USA  8.0  BED       7.0   12.0   7006.0
116  USA  8.0  CHAIR     7.0   12.0   6004.0
117  USA  8.0  DESK      7.0   12.0   5141.0
118  USA  8.0  SOFA      7.0   12.0   3837.0
119  USA  8.0  TABLE     7.0   12.0   5570.0

[120 rows x 6 columns]
```

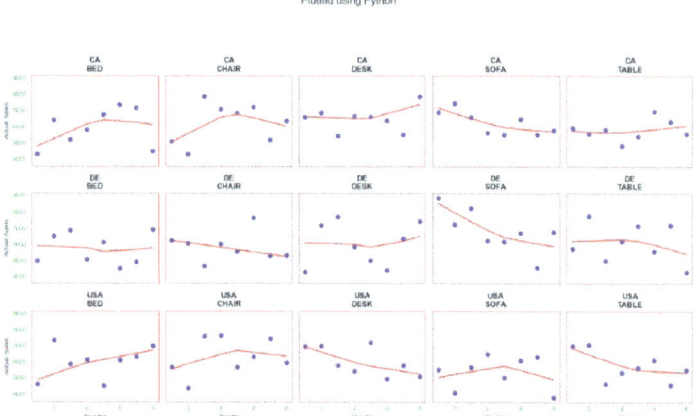

Conclusions

- R and Python program statements can be included in all Altair SLC programs using PROC R and PROC PYTHON, respectively. SAS software requires a SAS/IML licence to include R programming.

- SAS Viya includes access to both R and Python, but only R can be used directly in SAS 9.4. However, PROC FCMP could be used to add a Python connection to SAS 9.4M6 or later, using similar techniques to the first example in this chapter.

- Altair SLC includes PROC R and PROC PYTHON that can read SAS data sets directly into R and Python programs, provided the required R packages and Python libraries have been previously installed.

- SAS and R do not require statements to start in column 1, but Python requires that they do!

- PROC R automatically sends all output to ODS destinations, but PROC PYTHON only sends text-based outputs to ODS destinations by default, and requires the **wpsgloc** location to send image files to ODS destinations.

- Also PROC PYTHON may not output tables and graphics to the ODS destination in the same order as they are executed, so using OPTIONS PYTHONKEEP to keep the Python session running in the background, and adding ODS PDF STARTPAGE=NOW, will force them back into the expected order again.

- PROC R does not have the same problems with output order as PROC PYTHON, but does have an equivalent OPTIONS RKEEP, which will keep the R session running in the background between PROC R calls.

- SAS and R include LOESS smoothing, which can use multiple predictors, whereas Python includes LOWESS smoothing, which only allows a single predictor.

Recommended Reading

Web Links

- [Holland Numerics: Blog and Forums], **blog.hollandnumerics.org.uk**. Includes *VIEWS* News issues from 1998 to the latest newsletter for registered members on the blog site. These issues contain articles and links relating to WPS and Altair SLC.

- Altair Engineering, "Altair SLC 2025: New Features and Enhancements", **help.altair.com/2025/SLC/Altair-SLC-New-in-Release-en.pdf**.

- Altair Engineering, "Altair SLC 2025: Supported SAS Language Syntax and Reference", **help.altair.com/2025/SLC/Altair-SLC-Reference-for-Language-Elements-en.pdf**.

- Altair Engineering, "Altair SLC 2025: Using Python in a SAS Language Program", **help.altair.com/2025/SLC/Altair-SLC-Python-Procedure-User-Guide-en.pdf**.

- Altair Engineering, "Altair SLC 2025: Using R in a SAS Language Program", **help.altair.com/2025/SLC/Altair-SLC-Proc-R-User-Guide-en.pdf**.

- Altair Engineering, "Altair Analytics Workbench 2025: Creating and Running SAS Language programs and Workflows", **help.altair.com/2025/SLC/Altair-Analytics-Workbench-User-Guide-en.pdf**.

Alphabetical Index

2
2D Pie Chart...82

A
Altair SLC. 10-15, 20-22, 26, 33, 42, 47-49, 52-57, 59, 61, 64-66, 72, 78, 80, 82, 83, 90, 93, 99, 100
   AIX..12, 13
   Altair Analytics Workbench...11, 12, 20, 22-24, 28, 30, 31, 35, 37, 39, 40, 42, 44-46, 53
      Altair SLC Server Explorer..26
      Data Viewer..27, 34
      File Explorer...24, 27, 28, 31, 34, 35
      Home..28, 35
      Local Server..25, 32, 42
      macOS...23
      Output Explorer...24, 25
      Outputs..31, 32
      Project Explorer..28, 35
      Red Hat Enterprise Linux...23
      Results Explorer...24, 25
      SLC Servers..31
      Text Editor......................................24, 27, 31, 34, 42, 44
      Windows..22
      WPS Workspace.................................23, 24, 28, 30, 31, 35, 37-39, 53
   macOS..12, 13
   Red Hat Enterprise Linux..13
   VSCode extension..20
      settings.json...20
   Windows..12, 13
   Windows Server..12, 13
   wps..12
      -config..12
      -set...12
   z/OS..13
autoexec.sas...48, 49, 53

B
Box Plots...64

C

CDISC (Clinical Data Interchange Standards Consortium).........................47
    ADaM..47-53
        ADAE..52
        ADQS..52
        ADSL...52
        ADTTE...52
    DefineXML...47
    FDA..47
    metadata..47-50, 52
    SDTM..47, 49
clinical trials...47, 48, 53
CSV..83, 85, 86, 90

D

Data Steps...48, 53
    ATTRIB..50
    BY...85
    DATA...51, 84-86, 88, 91, 94
        VIEW =..84, 91, 94
    DO...85
    FILE...51, 53, 85, 86, 88
        LOG..88
        LRECL =...86
        PRINT...88
    IF..51, 85
        ELSE...51
        THEN...51, 85
    INFILE...88
    INPUT...88
    LENGTH..51, 84, 91, 94
    PRINT ODS =..
        FILE..55
    PUT..51, 85-88
    RETAIN...85
    SELECT...84, 91, 94
        OTHERWISE..84, 91, 94
        WHEN...84, 91, 94
    SET..51, 84, 85, 91, 94
    WHERE...51
    INFILE...88
    NULL...51, 55, 85, 86, 88

ODS 55

E

Eclipse IDE 11, 12, 22, 24, 28, 31, 35, 37, 39
Enterprise Guide 22
ERROR 48, 53
Error Bar Plots 61

F

FILENAME 51, 53
fork 47
Formats ....
   8 51
   BEST16 85
   YYQ6 .... 84, 91, 94
Functions ....
   CMISS() 51
   INTCK() 84, 91, 94
   MONTH() 84, 91, 94
   NMISS() 51
   PUT() 51, 84, 91, 94
   STRIP() 51

G

GIF 84
GitHub 47, 48, 52
   clinical-standards-data 47, 48
   clinical-standards-toolkit 47

J

Java 22
JavaScript 22
JPEG 84, 86-88, 90

L

LIBNAME 53, 84
   ACCESS = READONLY 49
   SAS7BDAT 26, 33, 49
   SD2 .... 26, 33
   V6 .... 26, 33
   V8 .... 26, 33
   V9 .... 26, 33, 49

WPD..26, 33, 49
Line Plots...57

M

Macro functions..
  %QUOTE()...85
  %upcase()..51, 52
Macro statements..
  %DO..52
  %IF...52, 85
    %THEN..52, 85
  %INCLUDE...51-53, 86
  %LET..85
  %MACRO..51, 85
  %MEND...86
metadata.source_columns..49-51
  algorithm..50
  format..50
  label..50
  length...50
  name...50
  origin..49
  origindescription..50
  table...50
  type...50
metadata.source_tables..50, 51
  keys...50
  label..50
  table...50

O

ODS..14, 83, 95, 100
  CHTML...14
  CSV..14
  CSVALL..15
  DOCUMENT..15, 16
    CLOSE...16
    NAME =..15
  ESCAPECHAR =...88, 91, 94, 98
  EXCEL..14
  EXCELXP...15
  GRAPHICS...14
  HTML...15, 16, 18, 19, 88, 89, 91, 94, 96

```
CLOSE..................................................................................................18
FILE =............................................................... 16, 88, 91, 94, 95, 98
GPATH =...................................................................... 88, 91, 94
NOGFOOTNOTE........................................................88, 91, 94, 95, 98
NOGTITLE..............................................................88, 91, 94, 95, 98
STYLE =.......................................................... 16, 88, 91, 94, 95, 98
HTML4...............................................................................................15
HTML5...............................................................................................15
HTMLCSS...........................................................................................15
LAYOUT.............................................................................................14
LISTING.............................................................................................14
MARKUP............................................................................................14
    TAGSET =.................................................................................14, 15
MSOFFICE2K....................................................................................15
ODS HTML.........................................................................................92
OLDLISTING.....................................................................................14
OUTPUT............................................................................................14
PACKAGE..........................................................................................14
PDF..............................................................................14, 89, 95, 96, 98, 101
    STARTPAGE = NOW..........................................................98, 101
PHTML...............................................................................................15
POWERPOINT.................................................................................14
REGION.............................................................................................14
RESULTS...........................................................................................14
RTF..............................................................................................14, 88, 89
    FILE =..........................................................................................88
    GFOOTNOTE...............................................................................88
    NOGTITLE...................................................................................88
    STYLE =......................................................................................88
TEXT..................................................................................................14
TRACE..............................................................................................14
XML...................................................................................................15
_ALL_ CLOSE...................................................................................89
ODS Graphics........................................................... 11, 54, 55, 64, 82, 83
    ODS Graph Templates..............................................................55
OpenDocuments..................................................................................
    LibreOffice................................................................................47
    OpenOffice.org..........................................................................47
OPTIONS...........................................................................................53
    NOFMTERR................................................................................85
    SASAUTOS =..............................................................................52
    SET =....................................................................................90, 91
    XSYNC................................................................................87, 90
```

XWAIT..87, 90

P

PhUSE (Pharmaceutical Users Software Exchange)....................................83
PNG..84
PROC COMPARE..52
    BASE =...52
    BRIEFSUMMARY...52
    COMPARE =..52
    CRITERION =...52
    ID..52
    LISTALL..52
    MAXPRINT =...52
    METHOD =..52
PROC CONTENTS...85
    DATA =..85
    NOPRINT..85
    OUT =..85
PROC COPY...15, 85
    IN =..85
    ITEMSTOR (Item Store)...15
    OUT =..85
PROC DATASETS..52, 84
    DELETE..52
    KILL...84
    LIB =..84
PROC DOCUMENT..15, 16, 18
    DELETE..18
    DOC...16, 18
        NAME =...16, 18
    LIST...16, 18
        LEVELS =...16, 18
    REPLAY..16, 18
PROC EXPORT..85
    DATA =..85
    OUTFILE =..85
    REPLACE...85
PROC FCMP..100
PROC FORMAT..85, 86
    CNTLOUT =...85, 86
PROC GANNO...55
PROC GCHART..54, 55, 67, 68, 79, 80, 82
    START =..80

PROC GCONTOUR... 54
PROC GMAP... 54
PROC GPLOT... 54-57, 59, 61, 65, 82
   ANNO =... 61
   ANNOTATE =... 61
   SYMBOL... 59, 82
      I =... 59, 65
      I = BOX00T... 65
      I = HILOTJ... 61
      I = NONE... 65
      I = R0CLI95... 59
      V = CIRCLE... 65
PROC GREPLAY... 55, 83
PROC GSLIDE... 54
PROC MEANS... 15, 19
   CLASS... 15
   DATA =... 15
   VAR... 15
PROC PRINT... 91, 94
   DATA =... 91, 94
PROC SGPANEL... 55, 82
PROC SGPIE... 55, 80, 82
   CATEGORYDIRECTION =... 80
   KEYLEGEND... 80
   START =... 80
PROC SGPLOT... 55-61, 63, 65, 67, 82
PROC SGRENDER... 55, 80, 82
PROC SGSCATTER... 55, 82
PROC SORT... 51
   BY... 51
   DATA =... 51
   OUT =... 51
PROC SQL... 48, 53
PROC SUMMARY... 84, 91, 94
   CLASS... 84, 91, 94
   DATA =... 84, 91, 94
   MISSING... 84, 91, 94
   NWAY... 84, 91, 94
   OUTPUT... 84, 91, 94
      OUT =... 84, 91, 94
      SUM =... 84, 91, 94
   VAR... 84, 91, 94
PROC TABULATE... 16

Alphabetical Index

CLASS...16
DATA =...16
TABLE..16
VAR..16
PROC TEMPLATE..55, 80
   DEFINE STATGRAPH..55
      CATEGORYDIRECTION =...79
      START =..79
   DEFINE TABLE..55
PSI Statistical Computing SIG...15
Python..10, 11, 22, 83, 93-95, 97, 100, 101
   Anaconda..93
   axes.flat..96, 99
   dataframes...93
   FacetGrid()..95, 98
   get_title()..96, 99
   import..95, 98
   LOWESS..95, 96, 99, 101
   lowess()..96, 99
   map()..95, 98
   matplotlib...95, 98
   numpy...93
   os..95, 98
   os.path.join()..96, 99
   pandas..93
   plot()..96, 99
   print()..95, 97, 98
   PROC PYTHON..93-95, 98, 100, 101
      DATA =...95, 98
      ENDSUBMIT...96, 98, 99
      EXPORT...95, 98
      PYTHON =..95, 98
      SUBMIT...95, 98
      TERMINATE...95, 98
   PYTHONHOME =..94
   PYTHONKEEP...98, 101
   savefig()..96, 99
   seaborn..95, 98
   set_axis_labels()..96, 99
   set_palette()..95, 98
   set_style()..95, 98
   set_title()..96, 99
   sort_values()..96, 99

split()...96, 99
statsmodels..95, 98
strip()..96, 99
subplots_adjust()...96, 99
suptitle()...96, 99
update()...95, 98
wpsgloc...95, 96, 99, 100

Q

Quality Control (QC)..53

R

R...10, 11, 22, 83, 84, 86-88, 90, 91, 94, 95, 100, 101
   environment variable...94
   grDevices...83, 87
      dev.off()...88
      trellis.device..87
   Hmisc...83, 87
      sasxport.get..86, 87
      sasxport.get()..83
   lattice..83, 87, 90, 91
      trellis..83, 90
      trellis.par.set()...87, 92
   library()..87, 91
   LOESS..95, 101
   print()..91
   PROC R...90, 91, 94, 95, 100, 101
      DATA =..91
      ENDSUBMIT...92
      EXPORT...91
      R =...91
      SUBMIT..91
      TERMINATE..91
   q()..88
   R_HOME..91
   RKEEP..101
   xyplot()..88, 92
   %exportlib..83, 85, 86
Regression Plots..59

S

S-plus..83
SAS Clinical Standards Toolkit (CST)..47

SAS Enterprise Guide..25, 32
SAS OnDemand for Academics..48
SAS Studio..22
SAS Viya..100
SAS/GRAPH...54-57, 59, 61, 64, 66, 82, 83
   DSGI..55
SAS/IML...83
SASHELP..54, 56, 57, 59, 61, 64, 66, 82
sashelp.class..54
sashelp.prdsal2..54
sashelp.prdsale..84, 90
SASHELP9...54, 56, 57, 59, 61, 64, 66, 82
sashelp9.class...54
sashelp9.prdsale...90, 91, 94
Scatter Plots..56

T
TITLE..16, 91, 94, 98

U
uninitialised variable...48, 53

V
Vertical Bar Charts..66
   Simple Vertical Bar Charts...67
   Stacked Vertical Bar Charts..68
Visual Studio Code Editor (VSCode)..10, 20

W
WARNING...48, 53

X
X...87, 90

www.ingramcontent.com/pod-product-compliance
Lightning Source LLC
Chambersburg PA
CBHW072149170526
45158CB00004BA/1561